# Eco 1

## Economics for
## NCEA Level One

# Eco 1

## Economics for NCEA Level One

Kelly Bigwood
Anne Younger

NELSON
CENGAGE Learning

Australia • Brazil • Japan • Korea • Mexico • Singapore • Spain • United Kingdom • United States

**Eco 1   Economics for NCEA Level One**
**1st Edition**
**Kelly Bigwood**
**Anne Younger**

Cover design: Cheryl Rowe
Text design: Cheryl Rowe
Illustrations: Cheryl Rowe
Proof reader: Sam Hill
Typeset: Cheryl Rowe, Macarn Design
Production controllers: Siew Han Ong and Jess Lovell

Any URLs contained in this publication were checked for currency during the production process. Note, however, that the publisher cannot vouch for the ongoing currency of URLs.

**Acknowledgements**
Photographs: Shutterstock

For product information and technology assistance,
in Australia call **1300 790 853**;
in New Zealand call **0800 449 725**

For permission to use material from this text or product, please email
**aust.permissions@cengage.com**

**National Library of New Zealand Cataloguing-in-Publication Data**
National Library of New Zealand Cataloguing-in-Publication Data

Younger, Anne.
Eco 1 / Anne Younger and Kelly Bigwood.
ISBN 978-0-17-019395-5
1. Economics. 2. Economics—Problems, exercises, etc.
I. Bigwood, Kelly. II. Title.
330.076—dc 22

**Cengage Learning Australia**
Level 7, 80 Dorcas Street
South Melbourne, Victoria Australia 3205

**Cengage Learning New Zealand**
Unit 4B Rosedale Office Park
331 Rosedale Road, Albany, North Shore 0632, NZ

For learning solutions, visit **cengage.com.au**

Printed in Australia by Ligare Pty Ltd
4 5 6 7 8 9 10 20 19 18 17 16

# Contents

ISBN: 9780170193955

ISBN: 9780170193955

# Consumer choices using demand

## 1 ▪ Consumer choice

**By the end of this unit you will be able to:**

- Define scarcity.
- Explain how the conflict between limited means and unlimited wants leads to the need to make decisions.
- Define choice.
- Explain how all economic decisions have an opportunity cost.
- Describe how different values influence the choices people and groups make.

Economics is a subject that will equip you with the tools to make informed decisions and to make better use of your own – and society's – resources. As an Economics student you will explore issues that impact directly on your life; personal choices, choices made by your community, and choices made by the government that affect you.

As individuals we make up a community, and our decisions affect each other. Economics is the study of how and why people make decisions and the flow-on effects of these decisions. By studying Economics we are able to participate more positively in our economy, make informed decisions and provide better economic management.

We will focus firstly on the choices made by individuals, such as yourself, and the household you live in.

ISBN: 9780170193955

# 1

Economics for NCEA Level One

# Scarcity

**Scarcity** is a fundamental concept in the study of Economics. We use the term slightly differently than the way we would in everyday language.

Scarcity occurs whenever people's **needs** and **wants** are greater than the means available to satisfy those needs and wants. It exists everywhere because our wants and needs are *unlimited* (we are never quite satisfied!). The means by which we satisfy our personal needs and wants are limited. Our 'means' are our **time, skills** and **money**.

This conflict between unlimited needs and wants, and our limited means or resources, results in scarcity. We are unable to have (or do) everything we desire because we do not have enough time, skills or money to get all that we want. Because of scarcity we have to make **choices**.

**Want**
What we desire to have but that is not necessary for survival, for example a Lamborghini sports car.

**Need**
What we must have in order to survive; food, clothing and shelter.

**Means**
Our personal resources we can use to satisfy our needs and wants; our time, skills or money.

1 Define choice.

2 Sometimes our family or whanau help us to gain the things we want and so can be included in our means. Describe a situation where your family or whanau has helped you to satisfy a need or want.

3 Describe a recent situation where you were unable to get what you wanted because you did not have the means, in other words, the time or skills or money. Identify the Economic term we use to describe this problem.

4 Think back to a time when you had to make a choice because of scarcity. For example, you were unable to buy both items you wanted so you had to make a choice.
   a Describe the situation, including details of what options were available.
   b Identify the choice you made and explain why you made that choice.
   c Identify the next best option or alternative, that is, the option you missed out on.

ISBN: 9780170193955

# Opportunity cost

In Economics, we consider the real cost of choices we make, which is more than simply the financial payment we make when buying a good or service.

Each time we make a choice we miss out on the next best option, in other words, there is always a next best option that we do *not* choose. This is a real cost to us, which we call the **opportunity cost**. All decisions have an opportunity cost.

> **Opportunity cost**
> The next best alternative foregone. That is, the second best choice that is not chosen.

As an example, let us assume you have $20 and that there are several things you want to do with it:

- A night at the movies
- Top-up your pre-paid cellphone
- Savings (piggy bank)
- Download an album.

Your means ($20 in this case) are limited. You are unable to buy everything you want, so you have to make a choice. After some careful consideration, you rank or prioritise your options:

1. Cellphone top-up
2. A night at the movies
3. Savings
4. Music download.

Your *choice* is to top-up your cellphone. The opportunity cost (the next best alternative foregone) is a night at the movies. The opportunity cost is *not* all of the other choices that you did not choose, it is the *next best alternative* that you did not choose.

1. Identify three possible flow-on effects of the decision to top-up the cellphone with the $20 in the case above. In other words, what might happen as a result of your choice?

2. Identify a possible opportunity cost for each of the following:
   a. Choosing to study Economics at university.
   b. Choosing to spend a year overseas doing volunteer work.
   c. Choosing to play netball every Saturday.
   d. Choosing a vegetarian diet.
   e. Going to a movie on Friday night.
   f. Choosing a sugar free diet.
   g. Buying a 12 month bus ticket to travel 2 km to school.

ISBN: 9780170193955

ISBN: 9780170193955

It is important to make choices wisely, using a sound decision making process. Choices may have **flow-on effects** to other people and other groups.

ACTIVITY

**1** Copy and complete the table below. List four options for spending your free time this weekend. List at least two advantages and disadvantages of choosing each option. Answer the questions that follow.

| Option | Advantages | Disadvantages |
|--------|------------|---------------|
| 1 | | |
| 2 | | |
| 3 | | |
| 4 | | |

**a** After weighing up each advantage and disadvantage, rank the four options from best to worst.

**b** Identify the option you have chosen and identify the opportunity cost (that is, the next best alternative).

**c** Describe a flow-on effect of your choice.

**d** Identify one possible way the decision could have a flow-on effect to another person or group.

**2** Austen works for an accountant, earning a salary with a net income of $2500 per fortnight. Her home needs a lot of renovating before she sells it. Austen has three options regarding the renovating: (1) She can renovate it herself on the weekends, but since that will take too long, she has decided to choose one of the other two options; (2) quit her job and renovate it herself, or (3) hire other people to renovate it for her.

**a** Identify the three options Austen has regarding the renovation of her home.

**b** Austen chose to give up her job and renovate the house herself. She is pleased because she does not have to pay someone to do it for her. Explain to Austen the true cost of the choice she has made.

**c** Describe one flow-on effect of the choice Austen has made.

**ACTIVITY**

**3** Copy the diagram below and use the words provided to complete it.

Limited     Time     Cost     Decision     Needs

Skills     Opportunity     Wants     Scarcity     Money

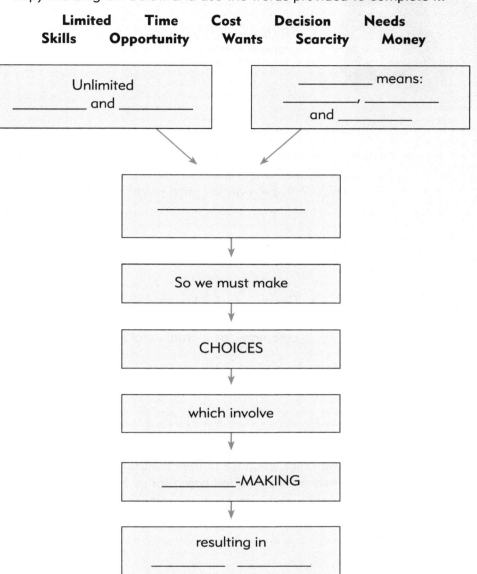

Unlimited _____ and _____

_____ means: _____, _____ and _____

_____

So we must make

CHOICES

which involve

_____-MAKING

resulting in _____ _____

## Values

Our **values** have a significant impact on our decision making. They are the principles and beliefs that we hold dear to us or what we consider to be important. Our values affect the importance we give to the costs and benefits when we are analysing our options.

The values we develop will be influenced by our peers, upbringing, cultural background, religious beliefs and the media.

- Guy values honesty, so he is likely to decide to give the money back if a shopkeeper accidently gives him more change than he was supposed to receive.

ISBN: 9780170193955

Economics for NCEA Level One

ISBN: 9780170193955

- Kathy values family, so she might decide to visit her sick grandmother rather than go to the movies with friends.

- Ngarimu is unlikely to ever buy herself pounamu (greenstone), as many Maori believe that the precious stone should only be given as gifts, never purchased for oneself.

- Destry is from Niue and values his cultural background, so decided to keep his hair long until his hair cutting ceremony, as is traditional in his culture.

- Lin's Chinese family may decide to have his grandparents move in with him, because in their culture older members of the family are valued and cared for by family, just as the children were looked after in their earliest years.

- The cast of Nicole's favourite TV show all wear their hair in a particular style, so Nicole has decided to get her hair done in the same way. The media has influenced her decision making, and what she considers important.

As members of a society we are obligated to uphold four key values:

1 Honesty.
2 Integrity.
3 Fair dealing.
4 Consideration of others.

Our values influence our decision making, which determines how we use our time, skills or money.

**ACTIVITY**

1 Define integrity.

2 Describe your cultural background or the culture that you identify with.

3 Explain one way in which your cultural background has influenced your decision making.

4 A 30 second television advertisement during the US Super Bowl can cost several million dollars.
   a Outline why firms would pay this much for a 30 second advertisement.
   b Draw a conclusion about what this huge cost indicates about the impact that the media can have on consumer decision making.

# 2 ▪ Consumer demand

**By the end of this unit you will be able to:**

- Define consumer.
- Define individual demand.
- Construct a demand schedule for an individual from given data.
- Draw a demand curve for an individual using given data.
- Illustrate and explain how a consumer will react to a change in price resulting in a change in quantity demanded.

## Consumers

A **consumer** is anyone who buys or uses goods or services. When you last downloaded music from iTunes, you were a consumer. When your parent or caregiver last purchased the groceries, they were a consumer. When you watched a movie on Sky TV, you were a consumer. All of the consumers in your home make up a household. All households in the economy make up what is known as the **household sector** of the economy.

ISBN: 9780170193955

ISBN: 9780170193955

Economics for NCEA Level One

# Individual demand

Take a moment to make a list of all of the things you can think of that you want. Let your imagination go wild … new clothes, your own room, a new car? Be specific about what you want; an iPod touch or perhaps an iPad, a 50-inch 3D TV, a beach house at Mangawhai, a world trip …

Now cross all the things off your list that you cannot afford. Is there anything left? In Economics, this is what we call a consumer's **demand**. In other words if an item is on your list of wants *and* you can afford it, then you demand it.

> **Consumer**
> An individual that buys or uses a good or service.
>
> **Individual demand**
> The amount of a good or service a consumer is willing and able to buy at a range of prices at a certain time.

Demand, then, is how much of a particular good or service you are both **willing** and **able** to purchase at a range of prices. It is important to note that price is the main factor affecting demand.

Let us consider Lily, who loves potato chips. At $2.40 she will buy one packet. If the shop had the same potato chips on special for $2.00, she would purchase two packets. If the price came down to $1.60, she would be both willing and able to buy three packets. Suppose it really was her lucky day and the price fell to $1.20. Lily would buy four packets of potato chips. At any price over $2.40, however, and Lily would go without her chips. They would be too expensive for her.

As the price falls, she is both willing and able to buy more packets of potato chips because she can afford to buy more – as long as everything else stays the same.

As the price increases, the quantity demanded falls because Lily cannot afford to buy as many as she could since her means are limited. This concept is called the **Law of Demand.**

> **The Law of Demand**
> As the price falls, the quantity demanded increases, *ceteris paribus* and vice versa.

*Ceteris paribus* is a Latin term which means 'all other things remain the same'. As the price falls, the quantity demanded will increase, as long as everything else remains the same. Other factors that could change this include income, tastes and fashions, or the price of other goods. We will address these in Unit 3. As long as these factors remain unchanged; the Law of Demand is true.

## Demand schedules

The demand data can be seen more easily on a **demand schedule**, which is a table that contains a person's demand information for a particular good or service over a range of prices. Have a look below at a demand schedule for Lily and her favourite potato chips.

**Lily's Weekly Demand Schedule for Sour Cream and Chives Potato Chips (180 g)**

| Price ($) | Quantity demanded (packets) |
|---|---|
| 1.20 | 4 |
| 1.60 | 3 |
| 2.00 | 2 |
| 2.40 | 1 |
| 2.80 | 0 |

We can see from the demand schedule that as the **price** increases, the **quantity demanded** decreases (as long as nothing else changes). When preparing the demand schedule, several key factors need to be included:

1. The title needs to include **who** the demand schedule is for, what the **product** is, and a **time frame**. These factors are important because information will vary depending on whose demand schedule it is, what the product is and whether we are looking at a quantity for a day, a week, a month or more.
2. The price column comes first and needs to specify whether the price is in dollar terms or cents. Prices can be listed in either ascending or descending order.
3. If you look at the schedule you will see that a change in price results in a change in quantity demanded. Quantity demanded is a term that relates specifically to changes in price, which is different to all of the other factors that affect demand.

**ACTIVITY**

Laura really loves *Smuggle* stationery. She is off to the shop to buy some erasers. At a normal price of $1.50 she would buy four erasers, however, when she arrives at the shop they are on special for half price. She decides to buy eight erasers. If the price had been $2.00, she could have bought two. Use this data to prepare a fully labelled demand schedule for Laura's monthly demand for *Smuggle* erasers.

ISBN: 9780170193955

# The demand curve

The information from the demand schedule can be used to construct a **demand curve**, which is a graph illustrating the amount of a good or service a consumer is willing and able to buy at a range of prices at a certain time.

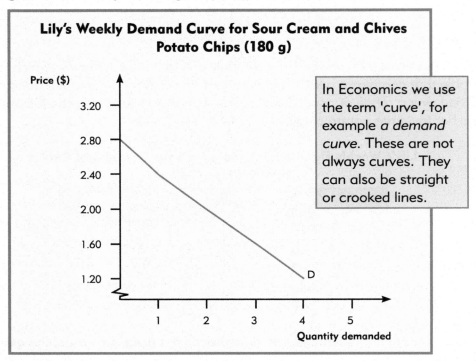

**Lily's Weekly Demand Curve for Sour Cream and Chives Potato Chips (180 g)**

In Economics we use the term 'curve', for example *a demand curve*. These are not always curves. They can also be straight or crooked lines.

When preparing a demand curve it is important that you remember to be TALL, that is, remember **T**itle, **A**xes, **L**ine and **L**abels. These skills are important in Economics.

- Include an appropriate **title**, as you would with a demand schedule. Include whose demand curve it is, what the product is, and a time frame.
- Ensure that the **axes** have an even scale. In the graph above, the graph size would not have been appropriate if it had started from $0.20, so the X axis is broken to show this.
- When plotting the points of the demand curve, make sure that the **line** starts at the first co-ordinates and ends at the last co-ordinates, and goes no further. Join the dots of each set of co-ordinates using a ruler. Make sure you plot the points accurately.
- Make sure that all **labels** are included, that the curve itself is labelled with a D, and that both axes are labelled.

A demand curve can be used to show how a change in price affects the quantity demanded.

ISBN: 9780170193955

The graph shows what happens when the price falls from $2.40 to $2.00.

At $2.40, Lily was willing and able to buy one packet of her favourite potato chips.

When the price fell to $2.00, the quantity demanded rose to two packets of potato chips. She was willing and able to buy more potato chips because she could afford more. Note how the effect of the price change is shown with dotted lines, labels: $P_1$, $P_2$, $Q_1$ and $Q_2$ and the arrows.

We use the term quantity demanded when we are describing a change in price. This is illustrated by a *movement along* the demand curve.

A decrease in **price** results in an increase in **quantity demanded**, *ceteris paribus.*

An increase in **price** results in a decrease in **quantity demanded**, *ceteris paribus.*

**ACTIVITY**

1 Explain the difference between want and demand.

2 Use the following demand schedule to construct a demand curve:

| Aroha's Monthly Demand for Movie Tickets | |
|---|---|
| Price ($) | Quantity demanded (tickets) |
| 7 | 5 |
| 8 | 4 |
| 9 | 3 |
| 10 | 2 |
| 11 | 1 |

ISBN: 9780170193955

**3** Copy the following demand curve graph and answer the questions that follow.

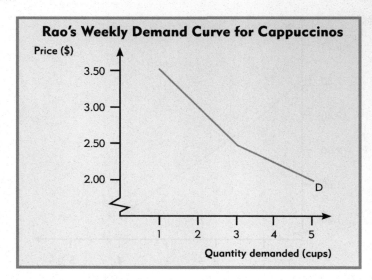

Rao's Weekly Demand Curve for Cappuccinos

**a** Use Rao's demand curve to construct his demand schedule.
**b** Show the effect of a price increase from $2.50 to $3.00 on your graph.
**c** Describe the change illustrated in your graph from question **b**.

**4** Copy the following demand curve graph and answer the questions that follow.

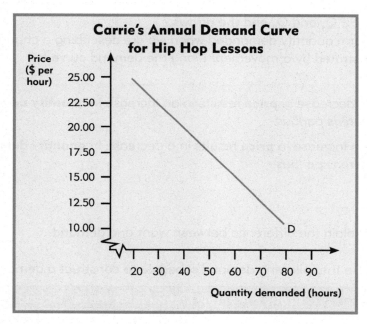

Carrie's Annual Demand Curve for Hip Hop Lessons

**a** Use Carrie's demand curve to construct her demand schedule.
**b** Show the effect of a price decrease from $20/hr to $17.50/hr on your graph.

ISBN: 9780170193955

**ACTIVITY**

**5** Copy the following demand curve graph and answer the questions that follow.

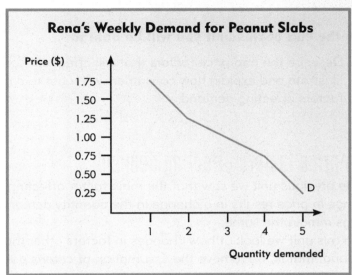

**Rena's Weekly Demand for Peanut Slabs**

**a** On your graph, identify the quantity Rena would demand at the current price of $1.00. Label it Q1.

**b** Show the effect of a 25% rise in the price of peanut slabs. Fully label the change.

**c** Explain why Rena's quantity demanded of peanut slabs falls as the price rises.

**6** Yazmin loves to drink soft drinks. If the tuck shop is selling them at $1.90 each, Yazmin will buy five per week. Over the last few weeks, however, the tuck shop has been offering soft drinks at special prices. As a keen Economics student, Yazmin noticed that she bought one more per week when they were $1.70 and another two more each week when they were $1.50. The week that the tuck shop charged $1.30 Yazmin was so excited she bought 10 and made herself ill. She was actually pleased to see the tuck shop increase its prices but this did not last long since as soon as the price rose to $2.50 she could only afford two cans.

**a** Use this information to prepare a demand schedule and a demand curve of Yazmin's weekly demand for soft drinks, using the price range from $1.30 to $2.50.

**b** Show the effect of the price of soft drinks rising from $1.30 to $2.50 on your graph.

**c** With reference to your answer to question **b**, fully explain the effect of the price of soft drinks rising from $1.30 to $2.50.

ISBN: 9780170193955

Economics for NCEA Level One

# 3 ▪ Changes in demand

**By the end of this unit you will be able to:**

- Describe the non-price factors that will affect consumer demand.
- Illustrate and explain how consumers will react to a change in non-price factors affecting demand.

## Non-price factors affecting demand

In the previous unit we saw that the main factor affecting demand is **price**. A change in price results in a change in the quantity demanded, as long as all other things remain the same.

In this unit we look at how changes in factors other than price might affect demand, that is, we remove the assumption of *ceteris paribus*.

- What happens to demand if the price stays the same, but tastes and preferences change?
- What happens to demand if the price stays the same, but the price of another similar good or service falls?
- What happens to demand if the price stays the same, but the price of another good or service that is purchased with it increases in price?
- What happens to demand if the price stays the same, but income increases?

## Tastes and preferences

Demand is affected when our **tastes and preferences** change. As an item becomes more fashionable we may be more willing to buy it. The opposite is also true, as our preferences move away from a good or service, we may be less willing to buy it.

Remember the definition of demand (the amount of a good or service a consumer is willing and able to buy at a range of prices). If tastes or preferences move in favour of a good or service, then demand increases. A new demand schedule needs to be produced, because the consumer is willing and able to buy more at the same price.

Consider the example of Jenna's demand schedule for shoes:

**Jenna's Annual Demand Schedule for Stretcha Shoes**

| Price ($) | Quantity demanded (pairs) |
|-----------|---------------------------|
| 60.00 | 4 |
| 80.00 | 3 |
| 100.00 | 2 |
| 120.00 | 1 |
| 140.00 | 0 |

ISBN: 9780170193955

If Stretcha Shoes became more fashionable, Jenna is likely to buy more of them at each price. Her new demand schedule may look like this:

### Jenna's Annual Demand Schedule for Stretcha Shoes

| Price ($) | Quantity demanded (pairs) |
|---|---|
| 60.00 | 4  6 |
| 80.00 | 3  5 |
| 100.00 | 2  4 |
| 120.00 | 1  3 |
| 140.00 | 0  2 |

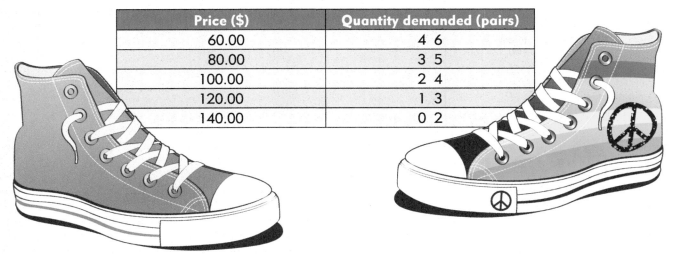

With the new demand schedule we can now create a new demand curve.

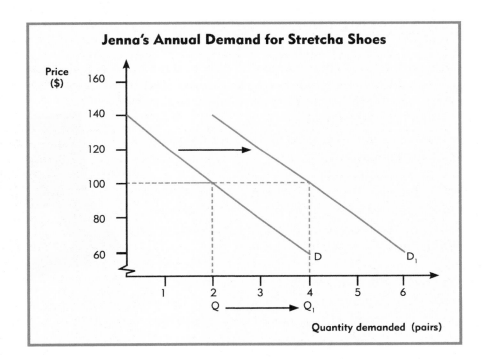

At $100, Jenna is now willing and able to buy more Stretcha Shoes. This increase in demand is shown by the demand curve shifting to the right. The new curve is labelled D1 to show that it is a new curve. The arrows and dotted lines show that at this price, Jenna is willing and able to buy more. Note also the differences in terminology:

- When there is a change in *price* there is a change in *quantity demanded*.
- When there is a change in a factor other than price (a *non-price factor*), there is a change in *demand*.

ISBN: 9780170193955

If Stretcha Shoes became less fashionable, then there would be a decrease in Jenna's demand for them. In this case the demand curve shifts to the left, as shown below:

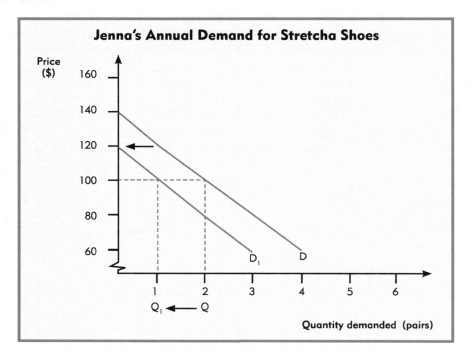

At the same price Jenna is now willing and able to buy fewer pairs of shoes – only one pair at $100.00 whereas before she would buy two pairs. Her demand curve shifts to the left and is labelled D$_1$ to show that it is different to the first demand curve.

Some specific examples of how our tastes and preferences could affect demand include:

1   Isobel has seen her best friend playing with a Nintendo dsi and is now desperate to buy one. Her friend has influenced her preferences and Isobel's demand for the product has increased as a result.

2   Neema has read recently that fish oil is supposed to improve memory and brain development, so her demand for salmon has increased. Her demand curve has shifted to the right.

3   Cameron recently became sick after eating too many Easter eggs and now he cannot stand the taste of chocolate. His preference for chocolate has decreased and so his demand has decreased also, shifting his demand curve to the left.

4   Joel has seen the latest skateboard advertised while he has been watching his favourite TV show. He thinks they look fantastic and has decided to buy one. The media has influenced his tastes and preferences, and has therefore influenced his demand for this good.

ISBN: 9780170193955

5   This winter has been particularly wet. There has been an increase in Madhurima's demand for umbrellas, shifting the demand curve to the right.

1   Bradley has an MP3 player that he was given when he was nine years old. Now that he is 14, he sees that many of his friends have an iPod touch. Draw a sketch graph of the likely effect this realisation will have on Bradley's demand for an iPod touch.

2   Elena is part of the championship grade netball team for her age. She thinks that an energy drink might give her more stamina for her Saturday game. Use a sketch graph to explain how this will affect her demand for energy drinks.

## The price of complementary goods

**Complementary goods** are goods that are traditionally used together, for example:

- A digital camera and a memory card
- A pot plant and a pot
- A computer and a printer
- A movie ticket and popcorn.

A change in the price of a complementary good will result in a change in demand for the other good. Assume for example that ceramic pots and pot plants are complementary goods. If the price of ceramic pots decreased, then the quantity demanded for these ceramic pots would increase.

ISBN: 9780170193955

Economics for NCEA Level One

Consider Steve's demand for ceramic pots, shown in the graph below. As the price of ceramic pots falls, Steve demands a greater quantity of pots.

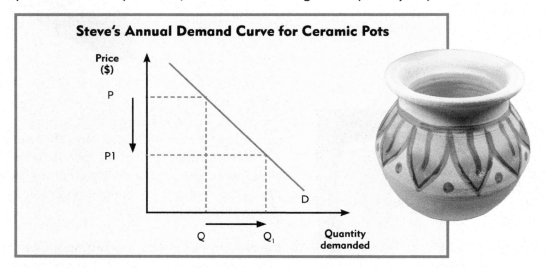

**Steve's Annual Demand Curve for Ceramic Pots**

Note the terminology: this *decrease* in *price* results in an *increase* in the *quantity demanded* from Q to $Q_1$ and a movement along the demand curve.

This also has an impact on the demand for pot plants even though nothing has happened to the price of them. Steve's quantity demanded of ceramic pots increased with the decrease in price – now he has to do something with all his pots! So he is likely to buy more plants to go in the pots. The ceramic pots and the pot plants are complementary goods – they are used together. The increase in demand for the complementary good (plants) is shown below.

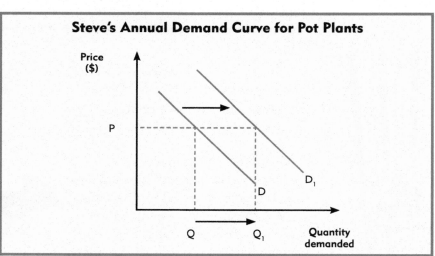

**Steve's Annual Demand Curve for Pot Plants**

ISBN: 9780170193955

**ACTIVITY**

1 Identify a complementary good for each of the following:
   a DVD                          b iPod
   c shoes                        d Nintendo Wii
   e toast

2 Rob and Suzanne love going to the movies. Use the demand model to fully explain what will happen to Rob's demand for movie tickets and popcorn when the price of movie tickets falls. You will need to draw two graphs; one for movie tickets and one for popcorn.

# The price of substitute goods

**Substitute goods** are goods which can be used in place of each other, for example:

- Coca-cola and Pepsi (though not everyone agrees!)
- Butter and margarine
- Popcorn and a choc top ice cream
- Tea and coffee
- Blu-ray discs and DVDs.

A price change in one of these goods will cause a change in the demand for the substitute good. Let us suppose that Carleena has a Blu-ray disc player which plays both Blu-ray discs and DVDs. If the price of Blu-ray discs falls, this will lead to an increase in her quantity demanded of Blu-ray discs.

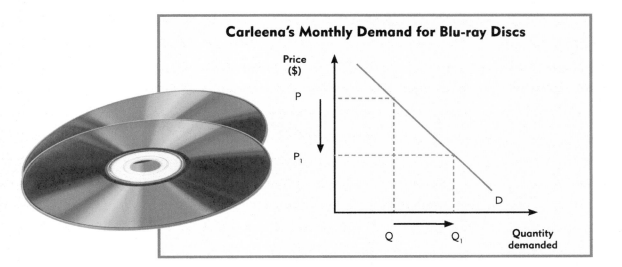

**Carleena's Monthly Demand for Blu-ray Discs**

As a result of this Carleena will demand fewer DVDs, since she will buy Blu-rays instead. The decrease in demand for DVDs is shown in the graph below.

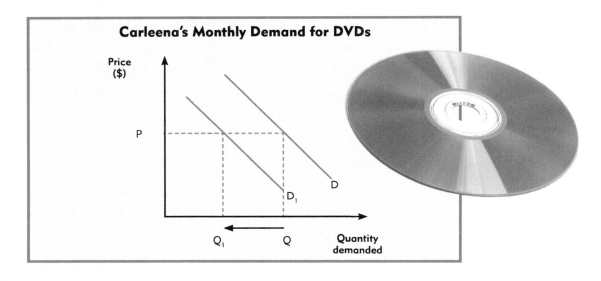

**Carleena's Monthly Demand for DVDs**

ISBN: 9780170193955

ISBN: 9780170193955

ACTIVITY

1 Explain the difference between a substitute good and a complementary good.

2 Identify a possible substitute good for each of the following:
 a sandals
 b pineapple juice
 c fish and chips
 d bike
 e Nintendo Wii

3 Jenny has three teenage sons who seem to be constantly hungry and really enjoy eating vegetables. Use the demand model to explain what will happen to Jenny's demand for frozen vegetables when the price of fresh vegetables increases.

# Income

**Income** is the funds received by a person or household, which may be earned (for example, a salary or wages), or unearned (for example, a benefit or an inheritance).

If a person's income increases, they are able to buy more of a good or service at the same price because they can afford to.

> **Income**
> Funds received by a person or household, which may be earned or unearned.

If the good is a **normal good**, the demand for it will increase when income increases, as the person is now willing and able to buy more at each price.

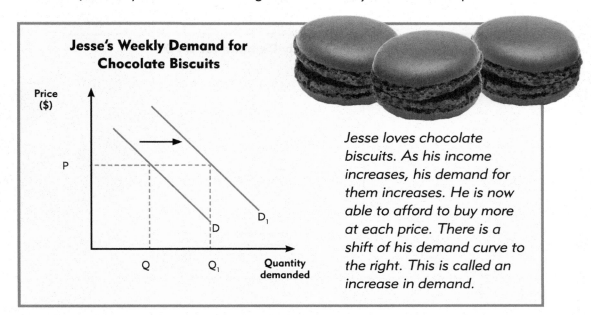

**Jesse's Weekly Demand for Chocolate Biscuits**

*Jesse loves chocolate biscuits. As his income increases, his demand for them increases. He is now able to afford to buy more at each price. There is a shift of his demand curve to the right. This is called an increase in demand.*

Chocolate biscuits are a normal good. This means that as income increases, the demand for a normal good increases.

There is another type of good called **inferior goods**. They are considered to be of a lower quality, goods that we use when we are on lower incomes. As our income increases, our demand for inferior goods will decrease.

This is because we are now able to afford better quality goods, the demand for which increases as our income increases.

While Jesse's demand for chocolate biscuits increased as his income increased, his demand for plain biscuits may have decreased. This means that the plain biscuits are an inferior good because his demand for them fell as his income increased.

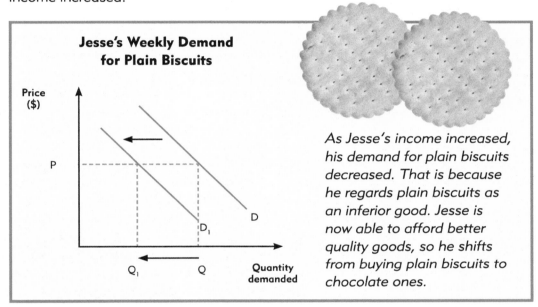

**Jesse's Weekly Demand for Plain Biscuits**

As Jesse's income increased, his demand for plain biscuits decreased. That is because he regards plain biscuits as an inferior good. Jesse is now able to afford better quality goods, so he shifts from buying plain biscuits to chocolate ones.

Nick can provide us with another example. When he was a student he would buy chuck steak for his flat, as this was a cheap cut of meat and he could afford it. After Nick graduated from university and started working, his income increased. As a result, Nick's demand for chuck steak (inferior good) decreased, and his demand for sirloin steak (normal good) increased. This is shown on the next two graphs.

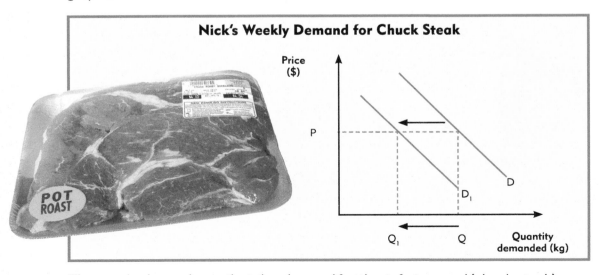

**Nick's Weekly Demand for Chuck Steak**

The graph above shows that the *demand* for the *inferior good* (chuck steak) *decreased* when Nick's income *increased*.

ISBN: 9780170193955

## Nick's Weekly Demand for Sirloin Steak

The graph above show Nick's *demand* for the *normal good* (sirloin steak), which *increased* as his *income increased*.

1 Classify the food below as either a normal good or an inferior good:
   - Sausage meat
   - Gourmet baked beans
   - Homebrand baked beans
   - Plain biscuits
   - Chocolate biscuits
   - Eye fillet steak.

2 Hezekiah usually makes his chilli with lentils as they are reasonably priced. He would prefer to make it with lean mince but it has been too expensive for him. Use the demand model to explain what happens to Hezekiah's demand for lentils when his income increases.

3 Luka was selected to play in a professional rugby team this season. His income has risen significantly. Use the demand model to show the effect of this on his demand for cereal (a normal good).

4 Use the demand model to show the effect of a rise in income on the demand for low cost shirts.

ISBN: 9780170193955

# Income tax

Personal income tax may impact on the demand for goods and services because it affects a person's **disposable income**, that is, their income after tax.

With more disposable income their demand may increase, shifting the demand curve for a normal good to the right.

The opposite is also true. If personal income tax rates increase, then there is less disposable income. This has the same effect as a decrease in income. Demand for the normal good will decrease and the curve will shift to the left.

> **Disposable income**
> Income after tax.

This flow chart will be useful when you are trying to determine the effect of any change.

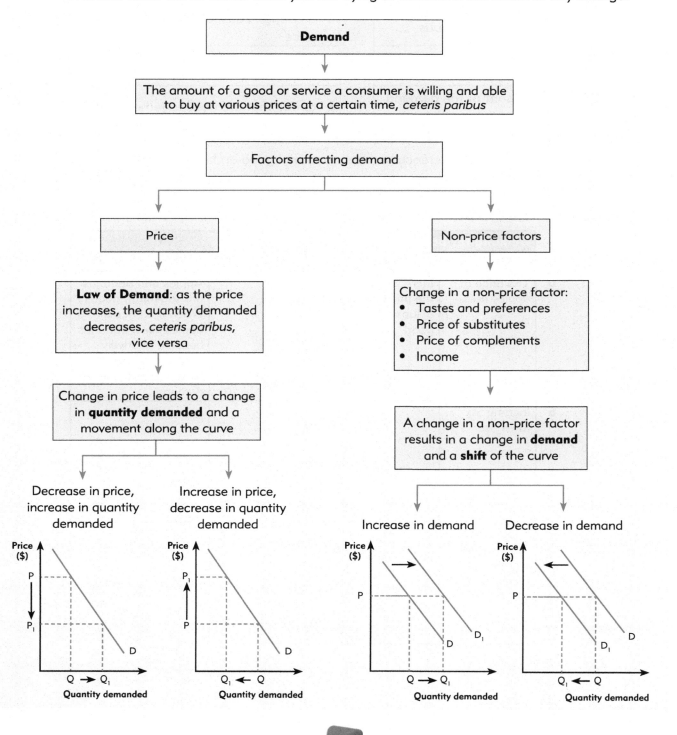

ISBN: 9780170193955

ACTIVITY

**1** Copy each term from column A and match it with the correct definition in column B.

| Column A | Column B |
|---|---|
| **1** complementary goods | **a** a change caused by relaxing the condition of *ceteris paribus* |
| **2** substitute goods | **b** the amount of a good or service that a consumer will be willing and able to buy at various prices |
| **3** demand | **c** goods that are used instead of another good |
| **4** *ceteris paribus* | **d** a change caused by a decrease in price |
| **5** movement down the demand curve | **e** all other factors remain constant |
| **6** shift of the demand curve | **f** goods that are used together |

**2** Explain the difference between a normal good and an inferior good.

**3** Copy and complete the Demand for Bananas chart below. The first scenario has been done for you.

| Demand for Bananas | | | |
|---|---|---|---|
| **Scenario** | **Factor** | **Graph** | **Explanation** |
| **a** The price of apples rises | Increase in the price of a substitute good | | Apples and bananas are substitute goods. When the price of apples rises, bananas become relatively cheaper, leading to an increase in demand |
| **b** Income tax rates rise | | | |
| **c** Bananas are found to be a great brain food | | | |

| Demand for Bananas (continued) | | | |
|---|---|---|---|
| Scenario | Factor | Graph | Explanation |
| **d** The price of bananas rises | | P, Q axes | |
| **e** Potassium is found to be causing liver damage. (Bananas are potassium rich.) | | P, Q axes | |
| **f** The price of oranges decreases | | P, Q axes | |
| **g** Secondary students are to receive government grants to supplement their income | | P, Q axes | |
| **h** The price of pancakes falls (and we love eating bananas with pancakes) | | P, Q axes | |
| **i** The price of bananas falls | | P, Q axes | |
| **j** The price of ice cream rises (and we also love banana splits) | | P, Q axes | |

ISBN: 9780170193955

ACTIVITY

**4** Copy and complete the Demand for Bacon chart below. The first scenario has been done for you.

| | The Demand for Bacon | | | |
|---|---|---|---|---|
| | **Scenario** | **Factor** | **Graph** | **Explanation** |
| **a** | Bacon is discovered to be a health food | Tastes and preferences move toward bacon | (graph with demand curves D and D₁ shifting right) | As bacon becomes more desirable there is an increase in demand and a shift of the curve to the right |
| **b** | Eggs fall in price | | (P/Q axes) | |
| **c** | Price of bacon rises | | (P/Q axes) | |
| **d** | New Zealand consumers find bacon too fatty | | (P/Q axes) | |
| **e** | | Price of a substitute falls | (P/Q axes) | |
| **f** | | | (P/Q axes) | There is an increase in quantity demanded. It is a movement down the demand curve |

ISBN: 9780170193955

**5** Copy and complete the chart below for the Demand for Organic Fruit.

| The Demand for Organic Fruit | | | |
| --- | --- | --- | --- |
| **Scenario** | **Factor** | **Graph** | **Explanation** |
| There is a huge advertising campaign for non-organic fruit | | 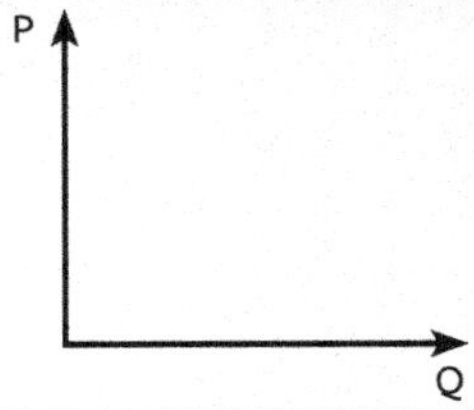 P ↑    → Q | |
| | Price of a substitute _____ | 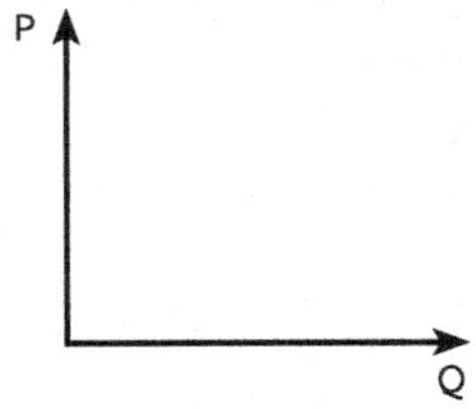 P ↑    → Q | This is an increase in demand. It is a shift to the right of the demand curve |
| New research on the potential negative effects of pesticides is released | | 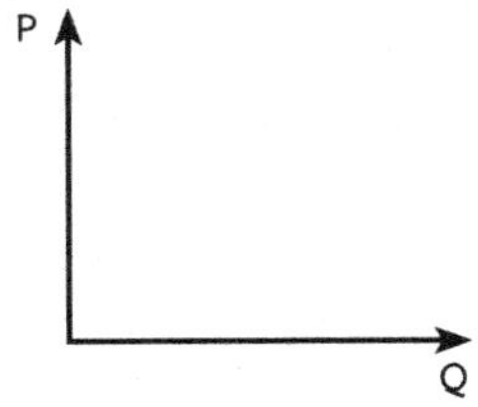 P ↑    → Q | |
| | Disposable income falls | 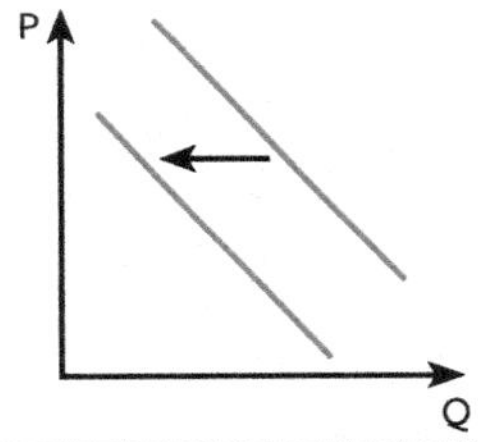 P ↑   ←   → Q | |
| Income tax rates fall | | 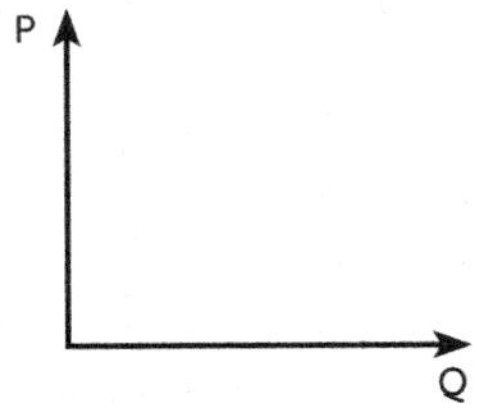 P ↑    → Q | |

ISBN: 9780170193955

**6** Copy and complete each graph and identify all of the possible reasons for each of the changes shown on the graphs.

**a**

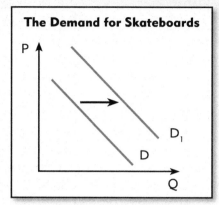

The Demand for Skateboards

**b**

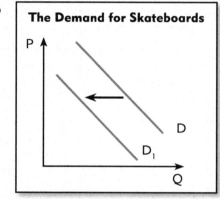

The Demand for Skateboards

**c**

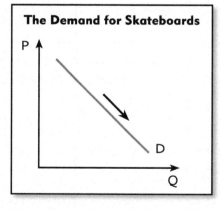

The Demand for Skateboards

**d**

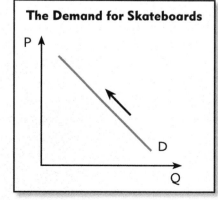

The Demand for Skateboards

**e**

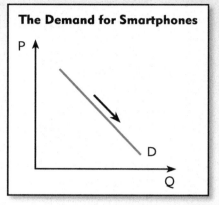

The Demand for Smartphones

**f**

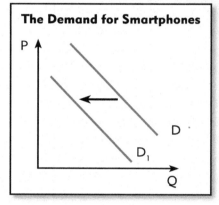

The Demand for Smartphones

**g**

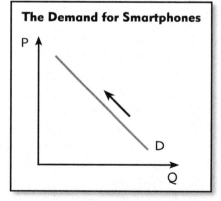

The Demand for Smartphones

**h**

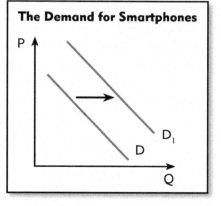

The Demand for Smartphones

ISBN: 9780170193955

**ACTIVITY**

**7** Copy each graph and identify all of the possible reasons for each of the changes shown on the graphs below.

**a**
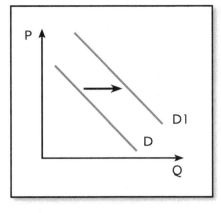

**c**
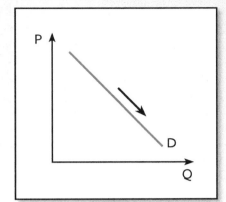

**b**
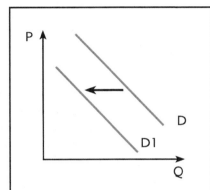

**d**
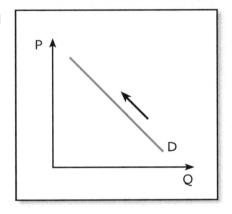

# 4 ▪ Household income and consumption patterns

**By the end of this unit you will be able to:**

- Explain relationships between household income and consumption patterns.

A **household** is a group of consumers who live under one roof. A household may consist of an individual, couples, parents or caregivers and their children, extended family, friends or flatmates.

The level of income a household earns has an impact on our demand for particular types of goods and services. As income changes, our spending (or consumption) patterns change.

When we earn an income, the first thing we will spend our disposable income on is **necessities**. These are the goods and services we consider to be essential for our survival, which include food, clothing (apparel) and shelter (housing).

At lower income levels there may be little disposable income left over after the basic necessities have been paid for. Paying for necessities takes up a much larger *proportion* of our disposable income.

ISBN: 9780170193955

As our disposable income increases we may decide to demand fewer inferior goods and instead buy better quality food and clothing, or improve our housing. We may be able to satisfy our basic wants, such as power, transportation, telephone, insurance and healthcare.

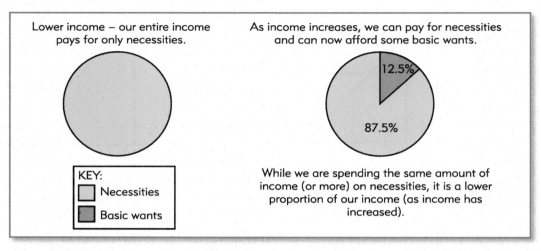

Lower income – our entire income pays for only necessities.

KEY:
Necessities
Basic wants

As income increases, we can pay for necessities and can now afford some basic wants.

12.5%

87.5%

While we are spending the same amount of income (or more) on necessities, it is a lower proportion of our income (as income has increased).

## Luxury goods

A household has only so many needs. Once our needs and basic wants are satisfied, then the demand for **luxury goods** increases. As income increases further we are able to afford luxury items such as cellphones, going to the movies, HD TVs, an iPad or overseas holidays. Luxury goods are certainly not essential for our survival (although some of us may think they are!).

At this point, with the higher income, we may be spending the same amount of income dollars on necessities, or even slightly more, but the *proportion* of total income spent on necessities begins to fall, and the *proportion* spent on luxury starts to increase.

## Savings

**Savings** is the proportion of income not spent. If household disposable income continues to increase, necessities are satisfied, and we have indulged in more luxurious goods and fewer inferior goods, then a greater *proportion* of household income may be saved.

## SKILLS

### Pie graph skills

- If figures are not given as a percentage, add all categories together to work out the total. Then calculate each item as a percentage of the total.
- Multiply each figure by 360 (the degrees in a circle) to give you the degrees of the circle that will represent each figure.
- Write a title for your graph.
- Draw a circle with a compass.
- Starting at 12 o'clock, use a protractor to mark the angles you have calculated above.
- Colour or mark each segment differently so as to distinguish them. Write a percentage on each segment.
- Include a key which identifies each segment.

ISBN: 9780170193955

1 The table below shows the percentage of New Zealand household expenditure in 1980 and in 2008. Use the table to answer the questions that follow.

| Group | 1980 | 2008 |
|---|---|---|
| | Percent | |
| Food | 19.70 | 17.83 |
| Alcoholic beverages and tobacco | 9.13 | 6.76 |
| Clothing and footwear | 7.30 | 4.48 |
| Housing and household utilities | 16.63 | 22.75 |
| Household contents and services | 9.17 | 5.26 |
| Health | 1.46 | 5.09 |
| Transport | 16.93 | 16.18 |
| Communication | 1.46 | 3.21 |
| Recreation and culture | 8.04 | 9.54 |
| Education | 0.36 | 1.78 |
| Miscellaneous goods and services | 9.80 | 7.12 |
| All groups | 100.00 | 100.00 |

(Source: www.stats.govt.nz)

**a** Classify each item on the table as either a necessity, basic want or luxury.

**b** Identify three significant changes between 1980 and 2008. For each change identified, give a possible reason for the change.

**c** If an average household's disposable income in 2008 was $1234, use the table above to calculate the amount a typical household would spend on:

   **i)** food                    **ii)** housing

   **iii)** transport             **iv)** clothing and footwear.

**d** Andrew has not studied Economics before. He looked at the table above and concluded that 'households spent less on food in 2008 than they did in 1980.' Explain to Andrew why this is probably not true.

**e** Prepare two pie graphs to show the percentage of household expenditure in 1980 and 2008.

**2** Write a 'breaking news' article explaining the relationship between household income and consumption patterns. Record it as a podcast, if possible.

ISBN: 9780170193955

# 2

# Producer decisions about production

## 5 ■ Producers

**By the end of this unit you will be able to:**

- Describe the individuals and groups who participate in the production of goods and services.
- Give examples of different types of goods and services.
- Identify various commercial and non-commercial goals of producers.
- Recognise that all producers make decisions, including choices regarding resource use, productivity, business expansion, goals and price and non-price competition.

### The producer sector

A **producer** is a particular individual or firm that supplies a good or a service. **Goods** are physical items such as furniture, computers or food. A **service** is when something is done for you, for example, a hairdresser provides hairdressing services, a teacher provides educational services, and an architect provides building decision services. All of the producers in an economy make up the **producer sector**.

It is important to distinguish between a **firm** and an **industry**. A firm is a *single* business or producer, for example *Bigwood Architects Limited*. An industry is a *group* of businesses or producers that produce a similar good or service, for example, the architecture industry (which is made up of individual architectural firms).

Within an economy, producers and consumers rely on each other. In Economics, relying on each other means being interdependent. The concept of **interdependence** is illustrated in a simple circular flow diagram.

ISBN: 9780170193955

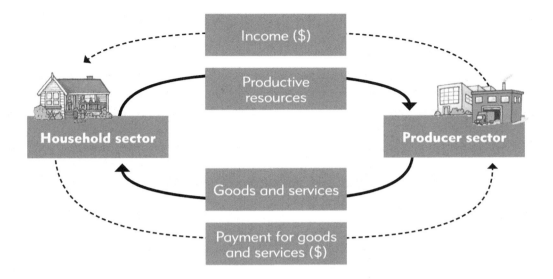

The household and the producer sectors are interdependent. They rely on each other.

Households rely on producers to provide goods or services to buy. This is shown by the direction of the arrows that indicate goods and services moving *from* the producers *to* the households. Households also need producers to employ them, so that they can earn an income and afford to pay for those goods or services. This is shown by income flowing *from* the producers *to* the households.

In much the same way, producers rely on households. Producers need to employ householders to work for them in order to make their goods or services. This is shown by the direction of the flow of productive skills and labour. Producers also rely on householders to purchase their goods or services, in order to generate an income for themselves. This is represented by the payment for goods and services flowing from the household sector to the producer sector.

**ACTIVITY**

Define the following terms:
a  good
b  service
c  firm
d  industry
e  interdependence.

## Types of producers

There are many different types of producers in our economy. We usually classify them as either **private** or **public** producers.

## Private sector producers

These businesses are owned by individuals or groups who come from the household sector. There could be many reasons why they are in business, for example:

- Make a profit.
- Gain a large share of the market.
- Be their own boss.

ISBN: 9780170193955

Economics for NCEA Level One

- Provide a good or service that they think should be available for purchase.
- The prestige of having their own business.

The main goal of private sector producers is usually to make a profit. The profit is the difference between the income earned by the firm and the expenses it has to pay. Business owner(s) hope that the income earned is a lot higher than the expenses paid.

Other private sector businesses are driven by the fact that they can see a need in the community and want to satisfy that need. These businesses are called **voluntary organisations**. Voluntary organisations are sometimes called non-profit organisations as their aim is to satisfy a need (and cover their expenses) and *not* make a profit. These businesses need income to cover expenses incurred in satisfying a need. Examples of voluntary organisations include *World Vision* and the *City Mission*.

**ACTIVITY**

a  List five private sector businesses that are likely to be in business to make a profit.

b  List five voluntary organisations.

# Public sector producers

Public sector producers are owned by the government, which sometimes provide goods or services that private businesses would not because they would not make a profit. Street lighting, for example, is a very desirable commodity, however, how would a private sector firm charge for the use of it? It would be very difficult. The government therefore provides street lighting, paying for it out of taxes. This is called a **collective good**, because it is provided communally out of taxes.

A government might also provide goods or services because they are considered beneficial for you, such as public education or public healthcare. Private education and private healthcare are often expensive and not everyone can afford them. The government considers that we should all have access to these services and so they are provided, again, funded by taxation.

Goods that the government or society consider beneficial for us are called **merit goods**.

# Government infrastructure

**Central government** refers to the elected representatives who meet in Parliament and the Beehive, and are concerned with New Zealand as a whole. Government departments such as the Ministry of Education, the Department of Conservation and Ministry of Health aim to provide goods and services to meet the needs of the community, rather than focus on profit.

Some of the goods and services provided by central government include public education, national parks, public healthcare, national defence and law and order.

As well as providing these goods and services the central government owns firms which are run

ISBN: 9780170193955

like private sector businesses, with a view to making a profit. These businesses are called **State Owned Enterprises**. To make a profit requires the firm to be efficiently run and accountable for its decision-making. The profit payments, called a **dividend**, are paid to the government, which is the owner or shareholder. Examples of State Owned Enterprises include:

* *Meridian Energy Limited*
* *Airways Corporation of New Zealand Limited*
* *New Zealand Post Limited.*

**Local government** officials and representatives are elected by local communities, for example, city councils, district councils and regional councils. Property owners pay rates to the local government so that they provide collective goods to the local community such as rubbish collection, libraries, playgrounds and parks.

## ACTIVITY

**1** Distinguish between private and public sector producers.

**2** Use your research skills to identify the names of six State Owned Enterprises.

**3** Name two government departments (or ministries).

**4** Explain the difference between the purpose or main goal of a government department and the purpose or main goal of a State Owned Enterprise.

## Goods

Goods are physical items that are used by consumers or producers. Goods can be further classified as **consumer goods** or **capital goods**.

**Consumer goods** are those physical items that are used by individuals or groups in the household sector. Examples of consumer goods include a bed, a PSP, a cellphone, a mirror or a lamp.

**Capital goods** are human-made goods which are used in the production of other goods and services. Capital goods are used by firms in the producer sector. Examples of capital goods include photocopiers, company cars, machinery or bulldozers. Certain goods are used as part of the production process and, while they may be finished goods, in themselves they are not of any use to anyone. A door, for example, is a

ISBN: 9780170193955

Economics for NCEA Level One

ISBN: 9780170193955

finished good but is not much use unless it is hung in a doorway. Goods like this are called **intermediate** or **semi-finished goods**. They are a type of capital good. Other examples of intermediate goods include car tyres, fabric, watch straps or a zip.

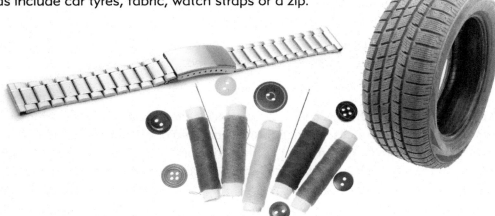

It is important to note that some goods can be both consumer goods *and* capital goods. What they actually are depends on the purpose they are being used for. A pen used in an office is a capital good, for example, but when Debbie is at home writing a phone message for her flatmate the pen is a consumer good. A computer in the office of a business is a capital good, but the computer at Mata's home that she does her homework on and plays games on is a consumer good.

## Services

A service is when something is done for you, such as a haircut, having private tuition, or when you see the doctor. There are several key service industries in the economy that businesses rely on, and that in turn rely on businesses for income:

- **Accounting industry** provides data about the financial performance of a firm.
- **Finance industry** provides funding or loans to firms.
- **Transport industry** moves goods from one place to another, by plane, road, sea or train.
- **Communications industry** enables firms to communicate with each other or with their clients through mail, email, internet, phone, mobile phone, conference calls or Skype.
- **Marketing industry** finds out what consumers want and how to get it to them. This includes market research, advice on selling price, packaging, distribution channels, promotions and advertising.

## Business choices

Throughout the following units we will see that producers come in many different shapes and sizes, that they have different reasons for being in business, and different motivations.

Each business has to make **choices**. What inputs will they use? Do they want to be a small or larger business? Do they want to become more efficient in their production methods and increase productivity (output per unit of input), and if so how are they going to go about this?

# Goals of a business

Many decisions will be strongly influenced by the reasons that their owners are in business, in other words what their goals are. Business owners may have commercial goals, such as wanting to maximise profits or increase market share (be the largest firm in the industry), or have non-commercial goals such as being in business because they love what they are doing, or because they want more job flexibility to spend more time with family.

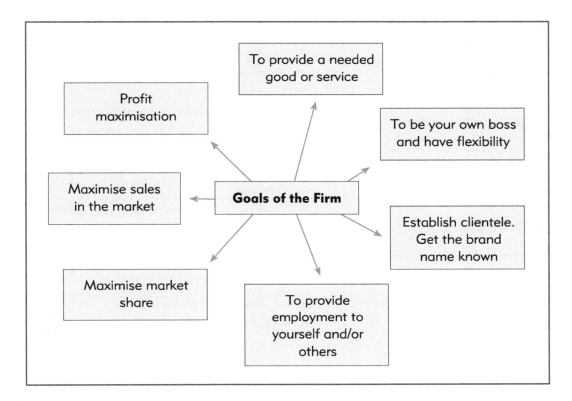

To provide a needed good or service

Profit maximisation

To be your own boss and have flexibility

**Goals of the Firm**

Maximise sales in the market

Establish clientele. Get the brand name known

Maximise market share

To provide employment to yourself and/or others

Goals of business owners may also vary according to how long they have been in business. A new business owner, for example, may just be looking to cover costs and survive (breakeven) until their brand name is established and the business has increased its share of the market. A more established business, on the other hand, may be more focused on profit maximisation.

Each choice that a producer makes will have consequences for the business, the owners and employees, as well as the customers and the community. Specific business choices and their flow-on effects are explored in the following units.

ISBN: 9780170193955

Economics for NCEA Level One

Copy the terms in column A and match them with the correct definition in column B.

| Column A | Column B |
|---|---|
| **1** intermediate good | **a** a single business or producer |
| **2** service | **b** goods the government or society consider beneficial for you |
| **3** profit | **c** goods are provided by the government out of taxation |
| **4** merit good | **d** a group of businesses that produce a similar good or service |
| **5** central government | **e** a human-made good used in the production of other goods and services |
| **6** collective good | **f** the reward to business owners, the difference between revenue earned and expenses paid |
| **7** capital good | **g** a finished good which is of little use until it is used in the production of another good |
| **8** firm | **h** when something is done for you |
| **9** industry | **i** elected representatives who make decisions for the country as a whole |

## Creating a mind map

A mind map is an imaginative tool which presents information in both an ordered and creative way. Mind maps are useful in the study of Economics. They allow us to categorise and sort data, make links and connections and explain content using colour and visuals.

Mind maps use both sides of our brain, activating both the left/logical side where we order information and the right/creative side where our brains process images and colour.

When preparing your mind map, make sure that:

- The central idea is in the middle of your page.
- Arrows link other ideas from the central idea.
- Each group of ideas has its own colour.
- Pictures and illustrations are used where possible.

For more ideas on mind mapping, search 'how to make a mind map' on YouTube.com. Tony Buzan, for example, illustrates the skill in his clips.

ISBN: 9780170193955

ISBN: 9780170193955

**ACTIVITY**

1 Distinguish between a capital good and a consumer good.

2 Explain how a cellphone can be both a capital good and a consumer good.

3 Identify four commercial and three non-commercial goals that business owners or managers might have for their business.

4 Explain the difference between a firm and an industry, and provide an example of each.

5 Identify five key service industries that businesses rely on.

6 Explain how these key service industries and other businesses are interdependent.

7 Identify three functions that a marketing firm might carry out.

8 Create a mind map encompassing the content of this unit.

# 6 ▪ Resources

**By the end of this unit you will be able to:**

- Define human, capital and natural resources.
- Define and identify examples of renewable and non-renewable resources.
- Describe ways in which cultural considerations impact on resource use choices.
- Explain the significance of sustainable resource use.
- Explain consequences of resource use choices on producers and society.

## Resources

Households and consumers use their means (time, skills, money) to satisfy their needs and wants. Means are personal resources, and include family or whanau.

Producers use **resources** to create the goods and services that are sold to households. Resources are sometimes called factors of production, might include the land that their building is on, the building itself, machinery used to produce the good or service, the staff, or the business owner who takes the risks and makes the decisions.

All of these resources are combined and used together to produce goods and services. These resources are the **inputs** into the production process.

Economics for NCEA Level One

## The production process

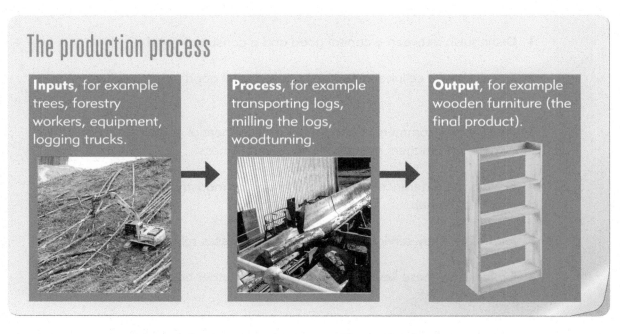

**Inputs**, for example trees, forestry workers, equipment, logging trucks.

**Process**, for example transporting logs, milling the logs, woodturning.

**Output**, for example wooden furniture (the final product).

Resources can be classified under three main groups: human, capital and natural.

## Human resources

Human resources are the people who contribute to the production process. They are grouped in two sub-categories; **labour** and **entrepreneurship.**

LABOUR

ENTREPRENEUR

1   **Labour** is the label we give to human work or effort, and also to the people who offer their services to businesses in exchange for **wages**. Labour resources include teachers, shop assistants, hairdressers, pipe fitters and lawyers.

2   **Entrepreneurs** are people who see potential for a business opportunity or they might have an idea for a starting a new business. The entrepreneur is the person who has started the business, has taken a risk and put their own funds into the business venture. If the business fails it is the entrepreneur who might lose his or her personal funds. If the business is successful, on the other hand, they will receive the profit. An entrepreneur is the risk taker and co-ordinates other resources in the business.

ISBN: 9780170193955

ISBN: 9780170193955

1 Explain the difference between labour and entrepreneurship.

2 Identify the payment that labour earns.

3 Identify the payment that entrepreneurs earn.

4 Yvonne has recently inherited $100,000. She will either buy a rental property with it, or start a business. Fully explain two possible consequences for *each* option.

## Capital resources

**Capital resources** are human-made goods that are used in the production of other goods and services, for example machinery, computers, or stationery.

As mentioned previously, intermediate or semi-finished goods are also capital goods because they are human-made and used in the production of other goods and services. They are goods that are complete but not of any use without being an input in another production process. A zip is an example of an intermediate good. It is a good in itself, but is of little use unless it is sewn into a garment such as a jacket or a pencil case.

## Investment

Capital resources are closely linked to **investment**, which is an important term in Economics. Here, investment means that a firm is increasing its stock of capital goods, in other words a business is buying more capital resources, probably to increase production.

In order to invest, in an economic sense, firms usually have to borrow funds in order to purchase capital resources, which may be very large and expensive equipment. Interest rates on loans are the cost of borrowing investment funds. This means that **interest rates** on loans are very important to firms that are considering investing. If interest rates are high, then it will be more expensive for firms to borrow in order to invest. If interest rates are lower, then it will encourage firms to invest as the cost of borrowing will be less.

Sometimes firms have to purchase more capital resources because the resources they currently own have worn out. When capital goods wear out we call this **depreciation**.

1 Define the following terms:
   a investment
   b intermediate goods
   c capital goods
   d interest rates

2 Describe four capital goods that a supermarket would use.

3 Explain the relationship between investment and interest rates.

4 Describe one example of investment that a producer might undertake for their orchard.

5 Josh, owner of *Electrics on Call*, has the option of borrowing in order to buy a new van for his firm. Outline possible consequences for Josh if he chooses to do this.

Economics for NCEA Level One

# Natural resources

**Natural resources** are 'gifts of nature'. They include anything which occurs naturally in the sea, on the land or in the air. Natural resources can be referred to as land, however, they can include water, trees, pounamu, sunlight, minerals, fish, birds and sheep.

Natural resources can be further classified into renewable and non-renewable:

1 **Renewable resources** are those that regenerate of their own accord within a reasonable time frame. This means they will regrow or reproduce as a natural process.

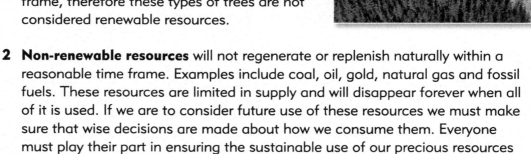

A tree, for example, produces seeds, then birds eat the seeds and deposit them in their droppings. The seed may then take again and grow another tree. The tree is a natural resource which has naturally regenerated.

Another example is wool, which grows back on a sheep after the animal has been sheared. Water naturally regenerates through the water cycle. Wind and the sun are also renewable resources and can be used to generate power.

The 'reasonable timeframe' part of this definition is important. A reasonable timeframe indicates that the resource will naturally regenerate faster than it is used, or well before it runs out. A pine tree, for example, can grow to full maturity (and therefore regenerate) in around 30 years. It is a renewable resource. Kauri or rimu, however, may take hundreds of years to naturally regenerate. Depending on how we utilise rimu or kauri, the trees could be used up before they have time to naturally regenerate. This is not considered a reasonable time frame, therefore these types of trees are not considered renewable resources.

2 **Non-renewable resources** will not regenerate or replenish naturally within a reasonable time frame. Examples include coal, oil, gold, natural gas and fossil fuels. These resources are limited in supply and will disappear forever when all of it is used. If we are to consider future use of these resources we must make sure that wise decisions are made about how we consume them. Everyone must play their part in ensuring the sustainable use of our precious resources so that they are available for future generations.

While certain natural resources do not naturally regenerate within a reasonable time frame, there are choices that producers and consumers can make to preserve them. To **recycle** means to use resources in another production process. Objects that may be recycled include aluminium cans, glass, paper and cardboard. By recycling we are protecting the natural resources that go into the production of those goods.

ISBN: 9780170193955

Another way that we can protect natural resources is to **reuse** them. Yoghurt pots, for example, when empty could be reused to grow seeds in. A plastic milk bottle could have holes punched in the lid and filled with water to use as a watering can. The jar that the pasta sauce came in could be cleaned and used to store homemade pickled onions. Each of these items is being reused for a purpose that is different to what it was originally designed for.

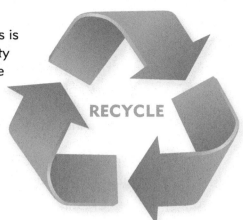

RECYCLE

## ACTIVITY

1 Use an example to explain the difference between renewable and non-renewable resources.

2 Identify one renewable resource that might be used by *Stenner Architects Limited.*

3 Identify one non-renewable resource that *Stenner Architects Limited* might use.

4 Distinguish between the terms recycle and reuse.

5 *Stenner Architects Limited* decide to purchase a fleet of electric cars instead of petrol powered cars. Fully explain possible consequences of this choice on the firm and on society.

## Sustainability

This is a point worth reinforcing. It is important that resources are used in a way to ensure they are available to meet the needs of future generations. Everyone has a role to play in achieving this, including producers. If producers choose environmentally friendly ways of producing their goods and services, they may find that their methods of production are more expensive, increasing their costs. Nevertheless the producer may also attract loyal consumers who appreciate and support them for making this choice to protect the environment.

The **Resource Management Act (RMA)** is a New Zealand law put in place to manage the use of natural and physical resources including land, air and water. Any person or firm wanting to build or develop is restricted in how they can use such resources. While sustainability may be reflected in the choices that producers make, laws like the RMA seek to ensure the sustainability of resources.

ISBN: 9780170193955

Economics for NCEA Level One

ISBN: 9780170193955

# Mines and quarries

New Zealand firms like *Stevenson*, that operate quarries for aggregate, and *Solid Energy*, the State Owned Enterprise that operates the Huntly coal mines, are two producers that utilise New Zealand's natural resources.

Initiatives they have implemented to reduce the environmental impact of their quarry and mining activities include:

- Creating ponds on old quarry and mine sites.
- Restoring land by planting grasses and native trees.
- Developing buffer zones where quarries and mines are surrounded by farming activity.
- Building visual screens such as the planting of trees to block unsightly quarries from residents, and to help regenerate natural bush.
- Installing water treatment and controls.
- Minimising dust by using encapsulators.
- Minimising noise levels by using acoustic shields.

For example, the site of one aggregate quarry in Mt Wellington that closed down in the 1990s is now the site of a residential suburb called Stonefields.

# Cultural aspects of resource use

'*Whatungarongaro te tangata toitü te whenua* ... People pass on but the land remains' (Maori proverb)

Indigenous people around the world traditionally have a strong link to the land and the resources that it provides. This is especially true of New Zealand Maori. In times past the land provided Maori with all of their basic needs in life; food, shelter and clothing. Many of New Zealand's natural resources have a cultural and spiritual significance to tangata whenua (people of the land).

The RMA has special obligations in relation to the Treaty of Waitangi and the principles of the Treaty must be considered when making decisions about managing the use, protection and development of natural and physical resources.

Resources of particular significance to Maori include:

- Urupa (burial sites).
- Wahi tapu (sacred sites).
- Archaeological sites.
- Flora and fauna, for example mahinga kai (food resources), or those used in raranga (weaving) or rongoa (traditional medicine).
- Areas of significance along the coast, for example, tauranga waka (canoe landing sites) and mahinga kai (food resources and gathering) areas.

ACTIVITY

*'Whatungarongaro te tangata toitü te whenua ...*
*People pass on but the land remains'* (Maori proverb)

**1** Explain how this proverb relates to the significance of sustainability for Maori.

**2** Use your research skills to describe what is meant by the term rahui. Explain how a rahui will affect the use of kaimoana (seafood).

## Resource combinations

Resources are combined and used in the production process in order for firms to provide goods and services.

**Inputs** (human, capital or natural resources) → **Process** (the resources are combined and processed) → **Output** (the finished good or service)

ACTIVITY

**1** Create a table with three headings: **Natural Resources**; **Human-made Resources**; **Human Resources**. Classify the following under the appropriate heading:

- climate
- nurse
- natural gas
- train tracks
- crude oil
- iron sands
- hammer
- stethoscope
- solar energy
- pilot
- waiter
- geothermal energy
- doctor
- menu
- welder
- truck
- plumber
- dairy owner
- deep sea fish
- Pacific Rose apple
- airport
- accountant

**2** For each of the natural resources you have identified above, use highlighters and a key to classify them as either renewable or non-renewable.

**3** Todd is an orchardist in Kerikeri. Explain why oranges are not a resource for Todd's business.

ISBN: 9780170193955

**4** Use the following diagram structure to identify 10 resources and any potential outputs for each of the following production processes. The first example has been done for you.

### SCHOOL PRODUCTION PROCESS

**INPUTS**
- teachers
- paper
- classrooms
- sports equipment
- hall
- pens
- whiteboards
- nurse
- fields
- library books

**PROCESS**
- School – Education

**OUTPUTS**
- education/classes
- sports events
- dramatic plays

**a** Fast food outlet

**b** Bakery

**c** Bus transport company

**5** Suggest at least one consequence if producers do not choose to support sustainable use of resources.

ISBN: 9780170193955

# 7 ▪ Productivity

## Production and productivity

**Production** is the process of transforming inputs into goods and services. We measure production as the total amount of output produced.

*John's Hydroponics*, for example, is a firm that grows hydroponic fancy lettuces and sells them to supermarkets. Total production is measured as the number of lettuces John grows over a certain period of time. In one month John's business produces 16 000 lettuces, therefore total production is 16 000 lettuces.

**Productivity** is a useful measure of a firm's performance because it takes into account the resources that were used to produce the output, such as how many workers it took to produce those fancy lettuces.

**Productivity**
Output per unit of input or the rate of output.

We can measure productivity in relation to labour (output per worker or labour hour), capital (output per machine), or land (output per hectare). Productivity is measured by dividing the output by the inputs.

**Productivity equals output divided by input.**

$$\text{Productivity} = \frac{\text{Output}}{\text{Input}}$$

Productivity has increased if:

- There is more output using the same input.
- There are fewer inputs required to produce the same output.

ISBN: 9780170193955

Economics for NCEA Level One

ISBN: 9780170193955

## John's Hydroponics

Let us assume that *John's Hydroponics* produced 16 000 lettuces in the first month, when John and one worker were the only labour resources involved.

In the second month John employed a third person to work with them and production increased to 21 000 lettuces. Production has increased from 16 000 to 21 000 lettuces.

But has production really been more efficient for this business? We need to look more closely at the firm's productivity:

**Productivity = Output / Input**
(Month One) 16 000 lettuces / 2 workers = 8 000 lettuces per worker
(Month Two) 21 000 lettuces / 3 workers = 7 000 lettuces per worker

Therefore while production has increased, the *productivity of labour* – the amount produced per worker – has actually fallen. They have been less efficient.

**1** Calculate productivity per worker in the following cases:

|   | Total production | Number of workers | Productivity per worker |
|---|---|---|---|
| **a** | 1500 pizzas per week | 12 | |
| **b** | 156 corkboards per week | 3 | |
| **c** | 36 building plans per year | 2 | |
| **d** | 56 coffees per hour | 2 | |

**2** Jacob and Bella own a small garage where they specialise in repairing and restoring old motorbikes. As demand for their services increased, they employed Edward to help with the restorations. Over time they also employed Sam, Jared and Paul. The following table outlines the productivity of the business as Jacob and Bella employed more staff:

| Labour Productivity for Bikes Repaired, per Month | | | |
|---|---|---|---|
| Month | Number of staff | Bikes repaired | Bikes repaired per worker |
| 1 | 2 | 10 | |
| 2 | 3 | | 6 |
| 3 | 4 | 28 | |
| 4 | | 35 | 7 |
| 5 | 6 | | 6.5 |

ISBN: 9780170193955

**a** Copy and complete the table by adding the missing data.

**b** Distinguish between production and productivity.

**c** Explain one possible positive consequence of an increase in productivity for Bella and Jacob's business.

## Labour intensive and capital intensive production

The way that a firm calculates productivity may depend on the methods of production they use.

**Labour intensive production** refers to a method of production where relatively more labour than machinery is used in the production process. Restaurants, for example, are labour intensive because they use relatively more labour (chefs, kitchen hands and waiting staff) than capital resources.

Labour intensive production processes are likely to use productivity of labour as a measure of productivity.

**Capital intensive production** refers to a method of production where relatively more capital resources than labour are used in the production process. Ice cream manufacturers, for example, use relatively more machinery than labour in their production of ice cream.

Capital intensive production processes are likely to use productivity of capital as a measure of productivity.

**1** Identify three industries that are likely to be labour intensive.

**2** Identify three industries that are likely to be capital intensive.

**3** Explain two advantages of capital intensive production over labour intensive production.

**4** *Fehi's Packaging* are changing their production process towards more capital intensive methods. Explain both potential positive and negative consequences of this change for their workers.

Economics for NCEA Level One

# 8 ▪ Productivity: Internal factors

**By the end of this unit you will be able to:**

- Describe internal factors that affect productivity such as technology, investment, specialisation and division of labour.
- Explain how each internal factor impacts on productivity, using data to support explanations.
- Explain potential consequences for the producer and for society of a producer's productivity choices regarding internal factors.

## Internal factors

Internal factors come from within the firm and are aspects that the firm has some control over. External factors come from outside the firm, and the firm has little or no control over them.

We need to analyse factors within the firm such as technology, specialisation, division of labour and investment, and look at how they affect productivity choices.

## Technology

Technology generally refers to the use of information or knowledge to solve problems. In Economics, technology also includes improved methods of production, which often involves capital goods. Machinery, computer systems and cellphones are all examples of **technology**.

As technology improves, productivity will usually improve as the *same workers are able to produce more output.*

**Technology**
Capital goods, processes and the methods of production that a firm uses.

There are many advantages to using technology:

- New technology is usually more efficient and works more quickly than labour, or older machines.
- Technology reduces the risk of human mistakes in the production process.
- Machines are able to work for longer hours than humans and each worker is therefore able to produce more output in the same time frame.

ISBN: 9780170193955

## CASE STUDY

### Instantaneous communication

Nick tests diesel pumps for a sprinkler company. If he comes across a problem with one of his pumps, he is able to use his cellphone to make a video call to head office to seek assistance and show them the problem.

This technology gives Nick the ability to carry out the job much faster than if he had to wait at the site for assistance to arrive and check out the problem first. Nick is therefore able to test more pumps per hour. His labour productivity is improved.

## ACTIVITY

1 Define the term technology.

2 Chris owns a lawnmowing and landscaping business. Explain how new technology could lead to increased productivity in his firm.

3 A firm that Riley works for has informed him that new technology is now able to perform the tasks that Riley normally carries out. Explain a positive consequence for the firm if they introduce this new technology. Explain one possible consequence for Riley.

## Investment

Investment has a special meaning in Economics – to buy more capital goods. It could be purchasing a new fleet of trucks, for example, or buying new equipment. More investment means increased capital goods which improve technology in firms, which will improve labour productivity.

> **Investment**
> To increase the stock of capital goods.

In order to invest, firms often have to borrow. Interest rates (the cost of borrowing) will have an impact on the amount of investment a firm chooses to make. *High interest rates* will increase the cost of borrowing and therefore make investment more expensive and perhaps less likely, whereas *low interest rates* make investment more affordable and so firms will be more likely to invest.

Remember:

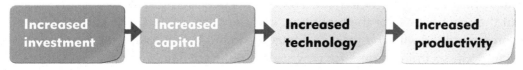

Increased investment → Increased capital → Increased technology → Increased productivity

ISBN: 9780170193955

Economics for NCEA Level One

ISBN: 9780170193955

1 Define the term investment.

2 Explain the link between investment and interest rates.

3 The Reserve Bank of New Zealand (RBNZ) has a huge influence on interest rates in New Zealand. Use your research skills to answer the following questions:
  a Describe the main roles of the Reserve Bank of New Zealand.
  b Identify the current Governor of the RBNZ.
  c Identify what OCR stands for.
  d Briefly explain what the OCR is.
  e Briefly explain how an increase in the OCR might have an effect on a business that wished to increase investment.

## Specialisation

To specialise means to focus on a particular area, which might be a task, a job or profession, a commodity or an industry. By focusing on a particular area or task, workers become better at what they do and produce more in a given time, in other words, increase productivity. Countries, regions, businesses, individuals or groups of workers may all specialise.

When a house is designed and built, for instance, many specialists are involved. An architect may design the house, a surveyor lays out the site, then builders, plumbers, electricians and painters each play their part in completing the job. Each specialist is skilled in their own area and can work more efficiently than an individual trying to complete all of the jobs themselves. The house will be built in fewer labour hours than if it was being built by a 'Jack of all trades'.

> **Specialisation**
> To focus on a particular area of production.

## Division of labour

**Division of labour** is when a production process is divided up into specific parts, and one person or group focuses on one particular task within that production process. Division of labour is typically seen in a factory production line. Division of labour leads to increased specialisation.

Instead of a single person building an entire car, for example, the factory will divide the job up into many parts and make each worker (or group) responsible for assembling one part of the car. Workers in each area become very good at what they do because of the repetition, and because workers with stronger skills become matched with the task. By focusing on the task it takes less time to learn how to do it, so training time for new staff is reduced. The workers may become innovative and create ways of making their task more efficient. It also means that workers do not have to shift between tasks, reducing downtime. Ultimately the whole task takes less time to result in a product (the good or a service). There is a larger quantity produced per worker, therefore, an increase in productivity.

There are, however, a few disadvantages with division of labour. Repetition can make the job monotonous, leading to staff becoming dissatisfied with their work. This could lead to a decrease in the quality of the work. If staff are unhappy at work they may leave the firm and new people will have to be trained, who may initially be slower at working. Because there is no one person who can complete the whole job, there can be problems if a staff member is absent and no one else is able to perform their job. There may be a holdup at that point (called a 'bottleneck'). These factors may lead to fewer goods being produced in the same time frame, and productivity may fall.

## CASE STUDY

### Division of labour in pin production

Who would have thought there was so much to manufacturing a pin? In his book *Wealth of Nations* (1776), Adam Smith describes how the division of labour could be applied to the making of a pin:

> 'One man draws out the wire, another straights it, a third cuts it, a fourth points it, a fifth grinds it at the top for receiving the head; to make the head requires two or three distinct operations; to put it on, is a peculiar business, to whiten the pins is another; it is even a trade by itself to put them into the paper; and the important business of making a pin is, in this manner, divided into about eighteen distinct operations, which, in some manufactories, are all performed by distinct hands, though in others the same man will sometimes perform two or three of them.'

Smith points out that by applying the division of labour principles to the pin factory there is an increase in productivity of somewhere between 240 and 4800 times!

ISBN: 9780170193955

Economics for NCEA Level One

**1** Define division of labour.

**2** Read the case study on page 59 and answer these questions:
**a** Assume there were 10 people working in the pin factory. Calculate productivity per worker per day, if they produced 20 pins in one day.
**b** After the implementation of the division of labour, output increased to 48 000 pins per day for the 10 workers. Calculate the new productivity per worker per day.
**c** Use the formula below to calculate the percentage increase in productivity with the new production method in place.

**Percentage increase**

$$\frac{\text{(New figure - old figure)}}{\text{Old figure}} \times \frac{100}{1}$$

**d** Imagine it is 1776 and you are a worker in the pin factory. It is your job to put the pin into the paper. Write a letter to your parents, who live in another country, describing your job and how you feel about it.

## Consequences

Firms have a certain amount of control over the internal factors affecting productivity. They can choose to invest and increase their stock of capital goods, determine their own production processes and decide whether or not to use division of labour. There are costs as well as benefits to each of these choices.

Investing requires the firm to spend funds that could be used for something else, such as wages for workers. If the firm must borrow in order to invest then it also needs to consider the cost of borrowing (the interest). This adds another expense to the business and will incur an opportunity cost.

Choosing to increase technology will increase productivity. This means that the cost of producing each unit may fall, leading to a decrease in price for the product and perhaps making the goods or services more competitively priced, leading to an increase in market share and increasing profit. Of course a lower price is good news for the customers too!

Improvements in technology can mean, however, that fewer workers are needed to produce the same output. This could lead to fewer workers being employed. As a result of this, the household sector may have less income and therefore spend less in the economy.

ISBN: 9780170193955

**ACTIVITY**

1 Sharda owns a hair salon in the centre of Christchurch. Her business is going well, but her goal is to improve her market share. She has come to you for some advice.

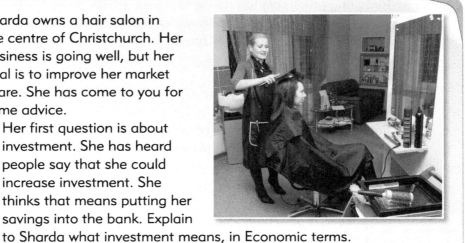

   a Her first question is about investment. She has heard people say that she could increase investment. She thinks that means putting her savings into the bank. Explain to Sharda what investment means, in Economic terms.

   b Another term Sharda has heard is division of labour. Explain to Sharda what this term means and how it could be useful in her business.

   c Explain to Sharda each of the ways that she could improve productivity in her firm.

   d It was recently announced by the RBNZ that the Official Cash Rate would rise, leading to an increase in interest rates. Explain to Sharda how this might affect her choices regarding investment and technology. Be specific and use data to assist your explanation.

   e Identify possible consequences of improving the productivity in this business (i) for the business, and (ii) for customers.

# 9 ▪ Productivity: External factors

**By the end of this unit you will be able to:**

- Describe external factors that affect productivity.
- Explain how each external factor might impact on productivity.
- Explain potential consequences of a producer's productivity choices, with regard to external factors, for the producer and society.

## External factors

**External factors** are issues that come from outside the firm. They are factors the business has little or no control over, for example:

- Legal
- Political
- Technological
- Environmental
- Cultural

## Legal factors

**Legal factors** refer to the system of law imposing certain conditions upon producers. Legal factors that could impact on productivity include:

ISBN: 9780170193955

- Requiring producers to provide four weeks holiday for each staff member per year. If staff are well rested they may work more productively, however, when staff are absent bottlenecks may appear in the production line. Other staff may need to be trained to do the work of staff who are on holiday, which will also hinder productivity.
- Parental leave regulations, which presently allow either parent to take unpaid leave from work for a period of time without forfeiting their position with the firm, have a similar effect. The worker's position is vacated only temporarily, however, new temporary staff may need to be employed and trained and this decreases productivity.
- New Zealand law presently regulates many workplace conditions including taking paid and unpaid breaks. Longer working hours could lead to an increase in production, since there are more hours available to produce output, however, producers are limited by law. However, the breaks may help the workers to work more efficiently when they return to work, increasing productivity.

## Environmental factors

**Environmental factors** are any outside influences that affect sustainable resource use and production impacts on the environment. Environmental factors include:

- Minimising the impact of production processes on the environment, such as pollution.
- Requiring sustainable resource use.
- Land restoration.

These requirements could decrease productivity because extra staff may need to be employed, or existing staff might have to undertake additional training. The firm is no longer able to focus solely on their primary production.

Environmental factors can improve productivity if firms invest in cleaner and more efficient processes and technology.

## Political factors

**Political factors** are those which may be imposed by a government or system of law, but differ from legal factors in that they are usually generated by a philosophical viewpoint or a social relationship.

Equal Employment Opportunity legislation is one example, which allows a wider range of workers (typically, women, the disabled and ethnic minorities) to access employment. Groups of people who may have had limited access to employment opportunities before the legislation was passed are now able to offer a range of skills to the business that may improve productivity.

## Culture

Staff may be unwilling to work on certain days due to religious or cultural beliefs regarding certain holidays, which has the effect of decreasing productivity. Cultural factors are considered in the requirements of the Resource Management Act. These requirements may restrict certain developments for firms limiting output and decreasing productivity.

ISBN: 9780170193955

## Technology

Technological discoveries made in the wider world may be able to be brought into the firm in order to increase productivity. Technology is wonderful when everything is going well, but so difficult when it breaks down. Firms that rely on outside assistance whenever there is a breakdown generally have little control over the time it may take to repair the equipment. Any delays can seriously hold up production and decrease productivity.

1  Define productivity.

2  Distinguish between internal and external factors affecting productivity.

3  Copy and complete the following table:

| Advantages of increased productivity | Disadvantages of increased productivity |
|---|---|
|  |  |
|  |  |
|  |  |

4  Outline the possible consequences on the workers if there is an increase in productivity.

5  Draw a mind map to summarise productivity choices of producers. Refer to page 44 for tips on mind mapping.

# 10 ▪ Economies of scale

**By the end of this unit you will be able to:**

- Distinguish between total cost and average cost.
- Define economies of scale.
- Explain specific reasons for economies of scale, such as technical economies, marketing economies and financial economies.
- Define diseconomies of scale.
- Explain the factors that cause diseconomies of scale.
- Explain how economies and diseconomies of scale can affect productivity.

## Costs

Before we investigate economies of scale and how it affects productivity choices, it is important to understand the language of costing.

**Costs of production** are the amounts paid by the producer to get the good or service ready for sale. Costs may include wages, rent, raw materials, packaging, interest and advertising. **Total cost** is the sum of all of the costs involved in getting the goods or services ready for sale.

ISBN: 9780170193955

This information is more useful if it is known how many units of production have been produced. **Average cost** of production is the cost per unit of output. We find the average cost by dividing total cost by output.

Once we know how much it costs to produce each unit we can determine the selling price which will be at a level that needs to adequately cover costs, make a profit and be competitive.

## The advantages of being big

If a firm becomes larger and its average costs fall, the firm is experiencing **economies of scale**. These are the benefits of being a larger firm. There are several reasons why firms are able to lower their average costs when the size of the operation increases.

As the scale of the business increases, total costs will increase. More inputs are required – larger spaces, increased materials, increased wages – but these total costs are spread over more output, leading to decreased average costs.

When there are economies of scale, there is a larger increase in output than the increase in the inputs. That is, while more resources have been used, there is a more than proportional increase in output. If there is a 5% increase in resources (inputs), but a 10% increase in production (output) as a result, then there are economies of scale.

> **Economies of scale**
> As the scale of operations increase, average costs of production fall.

Leah and Seth own a bakery where they make everything they sell. At the beginning of the year they were making 500 units per day (including everything from doughnuts to sausage rolls). The total cost of this daily production was $1 000. Over the next two years they increased the scale of their operations. They invested in new equipment, hired more staff and extended their premises. By this time production had increased to 3 200 units per day at a total cost of $5 500 per day.

**a** Distinguish between average cost and total cost.

**b** Calculate the bakery's average cost for both periods (at the beginning of year 1 and the end of year 2).

**c** Calculate the percentage change in average cost between the two periods of time.

**d** Suggest one possible reason for the change in average cost.

ISBN: 9780170193955

# Reasons for economies of scale

There are several types of economies of scale that illustrate how increasing the size of a business can lead to falling average costs.

- **Technical economies**

Businesses that function on a larger scale are able to benefit from a technical perspective. They are able to afford larger or more advanced (and more expensive) machinery to increase productivity. Smaller firms may be unable to afford such expensive machinery.

Some production processes require very expensive capital items, regardless of the quantity of output a firm produces. So an expensive piece of equipment could be needed, regardless of whether output is 1000 or 1 000 000 units. For the firm with the larger output the cost of using expensive equipment is lower *per unit of output (average cost)*.

When firms are larger they can often afford to carry out research and development, which may enable them to advance their goods and services and perhaps their methods of production. Larger firms are also able to benefit from mass production methods of production, such as division of labour, which increases productivity.

- **Marketing economies**

Many marketing costs such as advertising are fixed costs, that is, they stay the same regardless of the level of output. Larger firms are able to spread their fixed marketing costs over larger output, reducing the cost per unit.

Large firms require significant purchases of raw materials and other inputs. Because they are buying in bulk, firms can sometimes negotiate discounts from their suppliers. Once again, although the total cost of this purchase will increase the total costs of production, the *cost per unit* will fall.

These larger firms are also more able to employ staff who specialise in buying inputs for the best price. Once again, average costs fall.

- **Financial economies**

Larger firms have the benefit of being able to obtain loans more easily. Larger firms with more assets may be seen as more credit-worthy and less risky than smaller firms because they are likely to have been around longer and have a better credit history. Therefore their loans are more likely to be approved.

Because they are seen as less risky, large firms may be able to negotiate lower rates of interest on their loans and overdrafts. This too lowers average costs of production.

- **Managerial economies**

While the manager of a small firm needs to juggle all sorts of decision making about production, staff, marketing *and* finances, larger firms have the benefit of being able to afford to employ specialist managers who can focus on each of those particular areas. One person can be employed as a human resources manager to deal with staff, for example, and other individuals can be employed as marketing managers, production managers, finance managers and so on.

Larger businesses are likely to be able to afford to hire experienced and well qualified people for these roles. These people are likely to be more efficient because of their expertise, as well as being able to focus on their particular task rather than trying to perform a range of other roles.

ISBN: 9780170193955

Economics for NCEA Level One

Each of these factors increases productivity. Larger firms can usually afford to invest more in capital goods, research and development and improved technology. The size of operations allows specialisation of management and increased division of labour – two key internal factors improving productivity.

## Diseconomies of scale

If the scale of operations continues to increase, the firm can get too large and average costs may start to increase. This is called **diseconomies of scale.**

> **Diseconomies of scale**
> As the size of business operations increase, the average costs of production *increase*.

Management issues are the main cause of diseconomies of scale. As firms get too large, *communication* becomes more difficult as there are more layers of management to pass messages through and sometimes messages get mixed up. As a result, workers may not be so sure of what is required of them, which is likely to decrease productivity and increase average costs of production.

The *motivation* of workers may decrease as the large firm becomes less personal. Workers in big businesses may not feel as appreciated or may not see where they fit into the firm any more. If a large firm has implemented division of labour the workers may become bored with their work and lose sight of the significance of it. This has the effect of decreasing motivation, resulting in lower productivity and increasing average costs of production.

Management may have less *control* within big business as more and more tasks have to be delegated. When organisations become too large it becomes difficult to ensure that all staff remain focused on the same goals or to co-ordinate the different departments.

## Consequences

Economies of scale result in lower average costs. If the selling price stays the same it results in a greater difference between the revenue earned and the costs, that is, there is greater profit for business owners.

When average costs fall, the firm may decide to lower the selling price because they can afford to, at the same time keeping their profit margin the same. This makes their good or service more competitively priced – goods are cheaper for consumers – and because of the decreased price of their product the firm may attract more customers and increase its share of the market, in turn generating more revenue.

Diseconomies of scale, on the other hand, result in increasing average costs. The firm must choose to either lose profit, or increase their prices. This may result in less market share.

ISBN: 9780170193955

**1** Copy the term in column A and match it with the correct definition in column B.

| Column A | Column B |
|---|---|
| **1** economies of scale | **a** cost per unit of output |
| **2** average cost | **b** as the scale of operations increases, average costs of production fall |
| **3** technical economies | **c** specialisation of management as a result of increased size of the firm, and resulting in decreasing average costs |
| **4** total cost | **d** economies of scale resulting from promotional expenses being spread across greater output, bulk buying benefits and best buys because of specialised buyers |
| **5** managerial economies | **e** the sum of all of the costs involved in getting the goods or services ready for sale |
| **6** diseconomies of scale | **f** as the scale of operations increases, average costs of production rise |
| **7** marketing economies | **g** benefits gained in terms of borrowing due to the larger scale of production |
| **8** division of labour | **h** when a production process is split into many parts, each carried out by a different worker or group of workers |
| **9** financial economies | **i** lower average costs because of the use of machinery and production processes that large firms can benefit from |

**2** Explain the link between economies of scale and productivity.

**3** Fully explain how greater economies of scale could affect the profits of a firm.

**4** Draw a mind map on economies and diseconomies of scale. Use the information from page 44 to help you if necessary.

ISBN: 9780170193955

Economics for NCEA Level One

# 11 ▪ Business expansion choices

**By the end of this unit you will be able to:**

- Define and give examples of diversification.
- Explain why firms may diversify.
- Define and give examples of horizontal and vertical (both backward and forward) integration.
- Explain reasons why businesses may integrate horizontally or vertically.
- Analyse possible positive and negative consequences of business expansion choices on the producer, customers and workers.

## Business expansion

Economies of scale occur as a result of a business getting larger. Here we look at ways that businesses might increase their scale of operations through starting up, merging with, or taking over other businesses. We call this **business expansion.**

## Diversification

For a business to grow through **diversification**, it has to expand its business into something different. It has to add variety to what the business already produces. It may do this in various ways:

- Adding a new good or service to the existing range of commodities that it already sells, but aimed at a different market. A sewing supplies firm could start up another business that sells home cleaning products, for instance.

> **Diversification**
> Adding variety to what the business already produces, for example:
>
> **Sewing supplies** **+** **Cleaning products**

- Merging with or taking over an existing firm that is in a totally different line of business to the original firm. Suppose that Jack has an orchard and grows and sells oranges. If he was to diversify he might become a dairy farmer, or perhaps run a Bed and Breakfast from his home.

The key point of diversification is that the business is now dealing with a different good or service from the existing or original product line.

ISBN: 9780170193955

**ACTIVITY**

Suggest a good or a service that the following producers could potentially diversify into:

|   | Current business | A business it could diversify into |
|---|---|---|
| a | Pratima's Publishing | |
| b | The $3 Shop | |
| c | Dorothy's Second Hand Bookshop | |
| d | Homeopathy with Rose | |

Diversification can be useful for firms because it provides an additional source of income if there is a downturn in the original market, in other words, it is a way of spreading the risk. If the market for oranges becomes less profitable, or Jack's oranges are damaged in a terrible storm one year, then he still has dairy farming or the Bed and Breakfast business to rely on for income.

Diversification can, however, bring some difficulties. The business owners or managers may not be familiar with the new business and lack skills for running it efficiently. Workers may be unfamiliar with the new business and productivity may actually fall as they have to retrain or work in areas that they are unskilled in.

While the business is expanding, it may not get the benefit of economies of scale since the two business are so different and may not share costs.

**ACTIVITY**

1  Copy and complete the following chart:

| Diversification | |
|---|---|
| Advantages | Disadvantages |
| | |
| | |
| | |

2  Use the phrase *'don't put all of your eggs in one basket'* to explain the main benefit of expanding through diversification.

ISBN: 9780170193955

Economics for NCEA Level One

# Integration

Firms can also expand through integration. To **integrate** means to join with an existing business, which is related in some way to the original business. *Diversify* means to start up or join with a business which is different to the existing business. To *integrate* means that the new business needs to be *related* in some way to the original business, such as a competitor, or a supplier.

> **Integration**
> To merge with or take over another business which is in some way related to the original business.

To **merge** usually means that two businesses mutually agree to join together for the benefit of both parties. A **takeover** is where one dominant firm buys a share in another firm and the benefit is not necessarily mutual.

There are two forms of integration: **horizontal** and **vertical**.

## Horizontal integration

**Horizontal integration** is when a firm merges with, or takes over, an existing business that is at the *same stage of the production process*. Basically, it merges with or takes over a competitor.

An example of horizontal integration would be if the owner of one supermarket chain decided to merge with another supermarket chain.

Advantages of horizontal integration for firms include:

- Eliminating competition
- Increasing market share
- Increasing the size of operations and being able to experience economies of scale, such as buying in bulk, specialised management, division of labour *or* spreading overhead costs over a larger output
- Sharing costs
- Combining expertise and skills (two heads are better than one).

The main disadvantage of horizontal integration is that it reduces competition, which keep prices higher for consumers. When firms are competing they need to ensure they offer good prices to the consumers and may try to compete in other ways such as providing great service. The integration may result in a doubling up of specialist staff, and some may lose their jobs.

## Vertical integration

When a firm merges with, or takes over, a firm in the same industry but is at a *different stage of the production process* it is integrating vertically, for example, taking over a supplier or a distributor.

ISBN: 9780170193955

Producer decisions about production

There are two sub-types of vertical integration:

### Backward vertical integration

When a firm merges with or takes over a firm at an *earlier stage* of the production process, for example, Dougal's hamburger chain takes over a large meat processing plant. The main advantage of this type of integration is that the firm gains control over the suppliers and therefore has control over deliveries, quality of materials and is able to cut out costs such as the profit margin that each supplier puts on their product. This can be a problem, however, if new competitors have trouble accessing raw materials.

**Meat processing plant**

*takes over*

**Dougal's Hamburgers**

### Forward vertical integration

When a firm merges with or takes over another firm at a *later stage* of the production process, for example a furniture manufacturer merges with *Furniture Town* (which sells furniture to the public.) Again, these firms are able to cut costs and improve profit margins. They will benefit from economies of scale, such as marketing economies and financial economies.

**Furniture factory**

*merges with*

**Furniture Town**

## ACTIVITY

1  Copy the term in column A and match it with the correct definition in column B.

| Column A | Column B |
|---|---|
| 1 diversification | a merging with or taking over a related business that is at the same stage of the production process |
| 2 merge | b starting, taking over or merging with a firm which is in a different type of business to the original business |
| 3 takeover | c when a dominant firm buys a share in another firm |
| 4 vertical integration | d taking over or merging with a firm which is in a related area of business but is at a different stage of the production process |
| 5 horizontal integration | e joining together with another firm for mutual benefit |

2  Fully explain how business expansion is likely to affect (**i**) productivity of labour, and (**ii**) profits of the firm.

ISBN: 9780170193955

Economics for NCEA Level One

**3** Maree and Nick Plummer own a small clothing firm called *Plummer Enterprises.* They recently decided to expand their business by moving into the market for gourmet cookware.

**a** Identify the name of this type of business expansion.

**b** Explain one reason why *Plummer Enterprises* might expand in this way.

Maree and Nick have an opportunity to merge with another clothing firm.

**c** Identify the name of this type of business expansion. Be specific.

**d** Explain two advantages that Maree and Nick could experience as a result of the merger you identified in question **c**.

**4** Identify the type of business expansion each of the following case studies illustrates:

| Case study |
| --- |
|  **a** Harry owns *Exquisite Espresso*, where they roast, pack and sell coffee. He plans to buy the business of a coffee bean grower. |
| **b** Cleo the clown has an entertainment business where she is hired out to entertain at children's parties. She has recently decided expand her business into party planning. |
| **c** Stuart is a dairy farmer who is going to merge with a neighbouring dairy farm. |
| **d** Stuart the dairy farmer is now starting a gift basket business. |
| **e** Flora grows flowers and sells them to florists. She has decided to buy her own florist shop. |

**5** Darren is a panelbeater who has the opportunity to take over another panelbeating business.

**a** Name this type of business expansion.

**b** Identify one consequence of this decision for each of the following:

| Affected person or group |
| --- |
| **a** Darren |
| **b** Workers at Darren's firm |
| **c** Workers at the new firm |
| **d** Customers |

ISBN: 9780170193955

**6** Create a fishbone diagram to summarise the key points of this chapter. Use the blank diagram below as a guide.

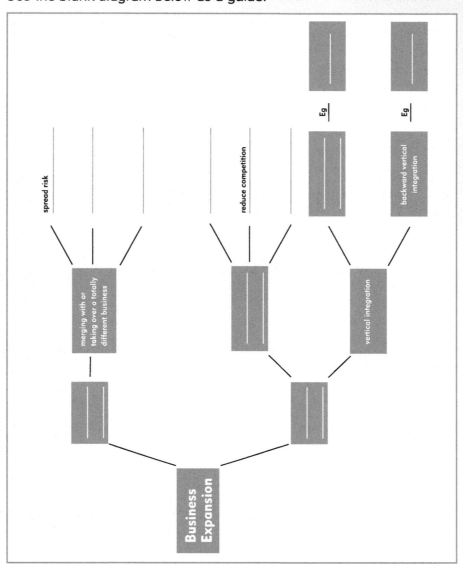

# 12 ▪ Price and non-price competition

ISBN: 9780170193955

**By the end of this unit you will be able to:**

- Distinguish between price and non-price competition.
- Identify examples of both price and non-price competition.
- Fully explain the advantages and disadvantages of price and non-price competition.

As there are often many producers of the same good or service, each producer must compete against the others to try to ensure consumers purchase from them. Producers need to choose how they will compete in the market.

There are two main methods that firms use to compete:

**1** Price competition

**2** Non-price competition.

Economics for NCEA Level One

# Price competition

Essentially, firms try to be the cheapest competitor. The biggest selling tool they can use is lower prices.

Some firms have built their reputations on always being cheaper than their competitors, and other firms use lower prices only occasionally such as during special sales. Price competition strategies that firms may use include:

- Discounts
- Sales
- Two for the price of one or 'Buy one get one free' deals
- Permanent lower price policy: 'We won't be beaten on price'.

**ACTIVITY**

Using your local newspaper collect a range of different examples of firms using price competition to sell their products. Find at least one example for each of the price strategies identified above.

**75% OFF** **EXCLUSIVE**

Firms are trying to maximise profits, and as lower prices increase the quantity demanded, firms hope that the increase in quantity will outweigh the lower price and lead to more profit.

| **Profit** | **Revenue** |
|---|---|
| Revenue minus cost. | Price multiplied by quantity. |

Firms which aim to be the cheapest often offer a no frills style of promotion. This will help keep costs down so prices can be as low as possible while still maximising profit. Compare the service of *Pak 'n' Save* (where you pack your own shopping) to *Countdown* (where checkout staff pack your shopping). *Countdown* will therefore require more staff and prices need to be higher to pay for them. *Pak 'n' Save* do not provide the same level of service so costs are kept down, meaning their prices can be lower.

# Non-price competition

Any method used by firms to compete which does *not* involve being the lowest priced competitor is non-price competition. These methods can be classified as product variation and product differentiation.

# Product variation

Product variation is making actual or real changes to the product. There are two sub-groups of product variation:

- Vertical product variation
- Modification of the product.

ISBN: 9780170193955

### Vertical product variation

This is when the same product is tailored to suit different income groups, for example airlines offer economy, business and first class travel on the same plane to the same destination, or car manufacturers offer a range of models, for instance BMW 520, 528, 535 and 550. Apple has the iPod shuffle, the iPod nano and the iPod touch. These are all examples of product variation.

### Modification of the product

This is when an improvement or an extra is added to a product to enhance its customer appeal. For example, a DVD player fitted into a car, fridges which beep when left open, cameras on mobile phones. Often over time these modifications become standard as all producers start incorporating them to stay competitive in the industry. For example air conditioning and radios were once rare in cars, now they are standard. Remote controlled TV used to be rare – now all TVs have them.

# Product differentiation

This is when a product is made to seem to be different without any actual changes being made. A range of techniques can be used to differentiate a product:

- Location
- Branding
- Sponsorship
- Loyalty schemes
- Gift with purchase.
- Packaging
- Advertising
- Service
- Competitions

### Location

A product is made to appear different because it is only available in certain places; for example top line brands of makeup are not available for sale in supermarkets. These firms are creating a sense of exclusivity about their products. Alternatively, the physical location of a business itself can give a firm an advantage. Locating a fashion store in a fashionable shopping area will mean it can access shoppers drawn to the general area by the cluster of other fashion shops. You often find restaurants grouped together for the same reason. Mechanics, tyre shops and other car related industries often cluster together so that customers can find them more readily. Location may also provide convenience thereby attracting more customers, such as a dairy near a high school.

### Packaging

The packaging of a product is used to make it more visually appealing. Perfumes, for example, are bottled in elaborately fashioned containers, or children's toys are often packaged in overly large boxes, making the product appear bigger and better.

ISBN: 9780170193955

Economics for NCEA Level One

## Branding

Branding is where a unique association or image for a product is created in the consumer's mind. The aim is to link the name of a good or service with the name of one firm's product, for example brand name jeans, or brand name cling film. Examples include denim jeans being referred to as *Levi's*, a sticking plaster being known as a *Band-aid*, or a photocopier being called a *Xerox*.

## Advertising

Advertising means promoting a product. The most common forms are Internet, radio, television and print media advertising where products are demonstrated or shown. Audio and visual elements, such as a jingle or logo, can be combined to reinforce the product in consumer's minds. Many websites provide advertising opportunities for firms.

## Sponsorship

Sponsorship is associating your product, for example, with a prestigious event or a celebrity. The popularity of the event or celebrity rubs off on your product, the result being that your product is perceived to be different from (and hopefully better than) other versions of the same product. An example of this are the ASB Classic and the Heineken Open tennis tournaments.

   A recent trend has been to associate the product with a charitable organisation, such as breast cancer research or natural disaster relief. Firms that do this promise to give a small part of the purchase price to a charitable organisation.

## Service

Service refers to all of the other things a firm offers customers as well as the product. These types of things include friendly and/or well informed staff, clean interiors, after sales support, availability of spare parts and replacements or delivery options. If two dairies are near each other, customers may choose to go to one instead of the other simply because of friendlier staff.

## Loyalty schemes

These are designed to encourage repeat sales. They work by giving rewards for more purchases, ranging from frequent flyer points offered by airlines through to coffee shop cards that give customers every tenth hot beverage for free.

ISBN: 9780170193955

### Competitions
Firms may offer a big prize to try to increase sales, entry to the competition being dependent on the purchase of a product.

### Gift with purchase
Firms may offer an extra product to entice customers, such as a t-shirt with a CD. Many cosmetic companies offer free samples of other products in their range with a purchase.

Regardless of the type of non-price competition, the cost to the firm rises. Prices will be higher. The only way a firm can hope to benefit from this is if the increase in quantity sold is large enough to offset the rise in costs.

## A summary of the types of price and non-price competition

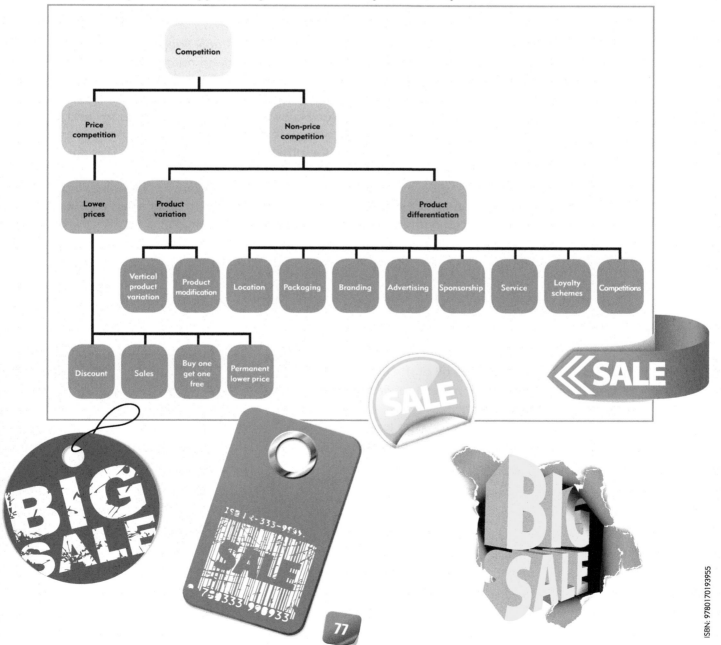

Producer decisions about production

ISBN: 9780170193955

Economics for NCEA Level One

## Advantages and disadvantages of competition

When considering the advantages and disadvantages of price and non-price competition it is necessary to consider both the consumer and the producer.

## Price competition

### Advantages

The main advantage of price competition to the consumer is that they can access the lowest price for a product.

It may allow producers to sell slow moving items and clear shelf space for products that are easier to sell or products with a higher return. Price competition can draw attention to your firm and help bring additional customers to your business. A sale can heighten consumer awareness of your business.

### Disadvantages

If firms are trying to make their goods or services as cheap as possible, consumers may not receive the same quality of product and/or only a limited range of products.

Since profit margins for producers are minimal, a high volume of products needs to be sold in order to offset small returns per item.

Price competition can lead to a **price war**. This will *only* happen when there are *few* firms in the market. (A few means a small enough number of firms that all consumers and all producers know what each producer is doing.) If one of the firms lowers its price everyone in the market knows. All consumers know and will buy from this firm. The other firms all know that the price has dropped and that they will most likely lose sales (revenue) if they too do not lower their prices. If the 'first' firm again lowers its price the others must all again follow. This can continue until the firms are selling their goods and services at a price below their costs. Some firms will not be able to do this and will close down. The remaining firms can put up their prices again but now have a greater market share as one or more of their competitors have been forced out of the market.

ISBN: 9780170193955

**CASE STUDY**

## Juice price wars

There are four juice shops in the mall: *Alice's Juice Shop, Barb's Juice Shop, Magenta's Juice Shop* and *Miracle's Juice Shop.*

One of the juice shops lowers its price and all of the others must lower their prices too, or risk losing customers.

The price falls too low for *Alice's Juice Shop* to keep operating and it closes. The other juice shops each have a greater share of the market now. The customers who used to go to *Alice's Juice Shop* now go to the other juice shops.

**CASE STUDY**

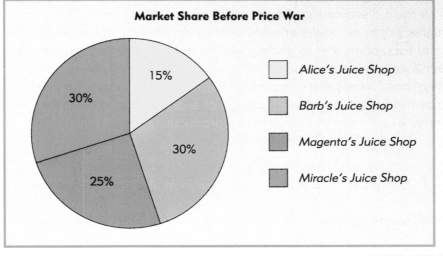

Market Share Before Price War

15% — Alice's Juice Shop
30% — Barb's Juice Shop
25% — Magenta's Juice Shop
30% — Miracle's Juice Shop

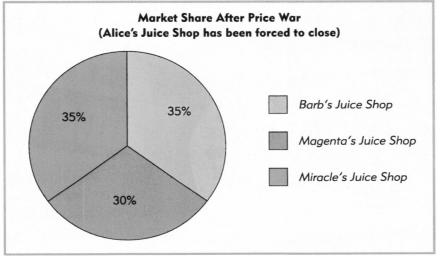

Market Share After Price War
(Alice's Juice Shop has been forced to close)

35% 35% 30%

Barb's Juice Shop
Magenta's Juice Shop
Miracle's Juice Shop

**Market share**
The proportion of total sales of the good or service that is made by a particular producer.

# Non-price competition

Non-price competition includes actual differences between products (product variation) and imagined differences (product differentiation). Whether the differences are real or not, firms are able to attract customers to their product at the expense of other producers. They may be able to gain market share.

### Advantages

When firms compete using product variation techniques, there is a wider range of products for consumers, including innovative changes and extras. There is little advantage to consumers of imaginary differences between products such as those created by advertising, however, consumers may enjoy better services or more convenient locations, for example. Producers are able to charge a higher price – this higher price may be greater than the increase costs incurred actually warrant – and despite the higher price they can increase the actual quantity of goods sold.

ISBN: 9780170193955

Economics for NCEA Level One

ISBN: 9780170193955

### Disadvantages

The main disadvantage of non-price competition is that consumers must pay higher prices as producer costs are higher. Product differentiation can make it hard for a consumer to discern which product is the best value – any differences between products are perceived and may not actually be real. As already mentioned, non-price competition results in higher costs for producers. Producers may not be able to take advantage of economies of scale if they are providing a range of different or differentiated products.

## ACTIVITY

**1** Explain why price wars only occur in markets with a few sellers.

**2** Identify five markets or products that have only a few sellers.

**3** Sort the following into either price or non-price competition:

**a** Liquidation sale

**b** Lease expired HUGE SALE

**c** Buy this CD and get the exclusive tour t-shirt

**d** Buy one and get 50% off the second

**e** A celebrity appearing in banking advertisements

**f** A hairdresser wins a hairdressing competition and is publicised in the local newspaper.

**g** ALL DVD'S HALF PRICE

**h** A man wears a sandwich board advertising pizza.

**i** Earn points with every purchase. Receive free gift with 500 points.

**4** Explain the difference between product variation and product differentiation.

**5** Classify each example of non-price competition in question **3** as either product variation or product differentiation.

**6** Provide four examples of generic products or services that are referred to by a brand name. Clingfilm, for example, is commonly referred to as Gladwrap.

**7** Describe your favourite television advertisement. Analyse how effective it is in terms of influencing you to buy the good or service.

**8** A friend of yours is a plumber. She sends you an email asking for advice because she is struggling to get customers due to the number of other plumbers in her area. Compose an email in reply, giving your friend comprehensive advice on how she might compete in this market. Be specific and ensure you fully explain the advantages and disadvantages of each option.

**9** Create a mind map to summarise the information in this unit. Refer to page 44 if you need help with this.

ISBN: 9780170193955

# Producer choices using supply

## 13 ▪ Supply

**By the end of this unit you will be able to:**

- Define supply.
- State the Law of Supply.
- Construct a supply schedule and a supply curve for an individual producer from given data.
- Use the supply model to explain how a producer will react to changes in the price of a good or service they supply.
- Use the supply model to explain possible flow-on effects of changes in quantity supplied.

## Producer

A **producer** is defined as any individual or firm that supplies a good or service. As we have seen, producers come in many shapes and sizes. They may have one owner, or thousands of owners (shareholders). They may produce a good or a service. The owners may be in business for many different reasons and have a variety of goals. They may be privately owned, or owned by the government. All producers have to make choices about production.

## Supply

**Supply** is the quantity of a good or service that a producer is willing and able to sell at a range of prices at a certain time, *ceteris paribus*.

Note the two key parts of the definition of **supply**– there has to be a *willingness* to sell, and the *ability* to sell.

There are many factors affecting the supply decisions of producers.

ISBN: 9780170193955

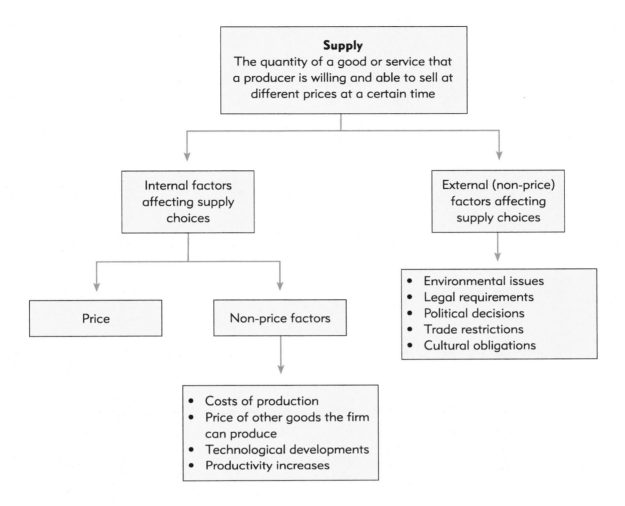

Internal factors are those that the firm has some control over, while the external factors are those that the firm has little or no control over.

We will look at each of these in turn. As you can see from the flowchart, the price of the good itself is an internal factor that is separate from all other factors. Price is treated differently in Economics. In this unit we are focusing on the way producers react to *changes in price*.

## Changes in price

Price is a very important factor in determining the production choices of producers. If the price they are able to sell their good or service at is high, then it becomes more profitable for them to supply those goods or services.

If the price of the good is low, however, then the producer may need to decide to use their resources to produce another good that is able to earn a higher price and therefore more profit.

This logic can be expressed in the **Law of Supply**.

**The Law of Supply**
As the price rises, the quantity supplied increases, *ceteris paribus* and vice-versa.

ISBN: 9780170193955

Remember that *ceteris paribus* means that this law is true as long as all other things remain the same. 'Vice-versa' means that the inverse is also true, in other words if the price falls then the quantity supplied falls, *ceteris paribus*.

## The supply schedule

A supply schedule is a table that contains a firm's supply information for a particular good or service over a range of prices. The Law of Supply can be shown on a supply schedule.

Here is an example of a supply schedule for the supply of pine framing timber from *Biland's Timber Yard* over one month.

**Biland's Timber Yard Monthly Supply Schedule for Pine Framing Timber**

| Price ($) | Quantity supplied (metres) |
|-----------|----------------------------|
| 2.00 | 100 000 |
| 3.00 | 150 000 |
| 4.00 | 200 000 |
| 5.00 | 250 000 |
| 6.00 | 300 000 |

We can see from the supply schedule that as the price increases, the **quantity supplied** increases (as long as everything else remains the same). Notice quantity supplied is the term that relates specifically to changes in **price**, and is different to all of the other factors that affect supply.

The following elements must always be included when preparing a supply schedule:

1 A **title** needs to include **who** the schedule is for, what the **product** is, and a **time frame**. These factors are important because the information will vary depending on who the producer is, what the product is (including the size in metres, kilograms and so on), and whether we are looking at a quantity for a day, a week or a month.

2 The price column comes first and needs to specify whether the price is in dollars or cents. Prices can be listed in either ascending or descending order.

**ACTIVITY**

1 Define supply.

2 State the Law of Supply.

3 Imagine you make picture frames decorated with sea shells and glitter. Explain why you would make more frames available at higher prices than lower prices.

ISBN: 9780170193955

# The supply curve

The information from the supply schedule can be used to construct a supply curve, which is a graph illustrating the amount of a good or service a producer is willing and able to sell at a range of prices at a certain time.

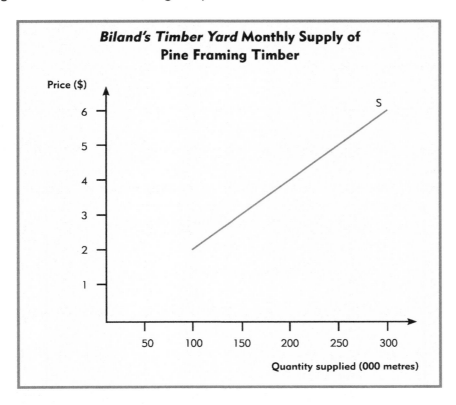

When preparing a supply curve it is important that you remember to be TALL, that is, remember **T**itle, **A**xes, **L**ine and **L**abels:

- Include an appropriate **title**, as you would with a supply schedule. Include the name of the producer, what the product is and the time frame.
- Ensure that the **axes** have an even scale. It may be necessary to show a break in the axes to ensure the scale is even. Note that in the graph above, 50 000 metres was not on the schedule nevertheless the measurement was included on the axis to ensure the scale was even.
- When plotting the points of the supply curve, make sure that the **line** starts at the first co-ordinates and ends at the last co-ordinates, and goes no further. Join the dots of each set of co-ordinates using a ruler.
- Make sure that all **labels** are included, that the curve itself is labelled with an S (for supply), and the axes are labelled. Note the reference to quantity supplied (000 metres).

ISBN: 9780170193955

**1** Use the following supply schedule to construct a supply curve.

| Plumbers R Us Limited Weekly Supply Schedule of Pipes | |
|---|---|
| Price ($ per metre) | Quantity supplied |
| 10 | 300 |
| 12 | 400 |
| 14 | 500 |
| 16 | 600 |
| 18 | 700 |
| 20 | 800 |
| 22 | 900 |
| 24 | 1000 |

**2** Use the following supply curve to derive a supply schedule.

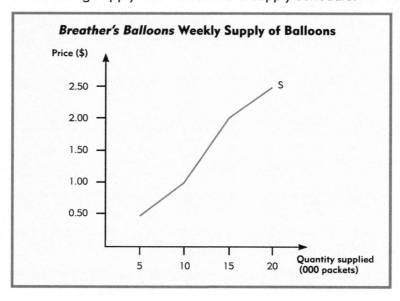

The supply curve can be used to show how a change in price affects the quantity supplied.

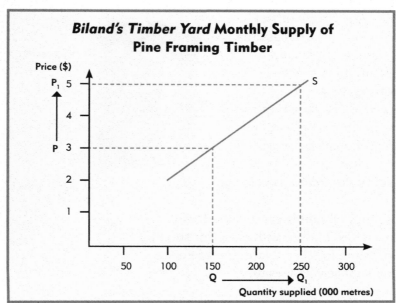

The graph shows what happens when the price increases from $3 per metre to $5 per metre. At $3 per metre the timber yard was willing and able to sell 150 000 metres of pine framing timber. When the price increased to $5, the quantity supplied rose to 250 000 metres. They are willing and able to sell more at the higher price because it is more profitable. This change in price resulted in a movement along the supply curve (from P and Q to $P_1$ and $Q_1$).

We use the term quantity supplied when we are describing the effect of a change in price.

An increase in **price** results in an increase in **quantity supplied,** *ceteris paribus.*

A decrease in **price** results in a decrease in **quantity supplied,** *ceteris paribus.*

## ACTIVITY

1 Use the following supply schedule to construct a supply curve and answer the questions that follow.

| *Rewi Ramikin's* **Weekly Supply of Macaroni Cheese** | |
|---|---|
| **Price ($)** | **Quantity (000 bowls)** |
| 20 | 4 |
| 15 | 3 |
| 10 | 2 |
| 5 | 1 |

**a** Show the effect of a price rise from $10 to $15. Fully label your graph.

**b** Calculate the change in quantity supplied.

**c** Show the effect of a price fall from $20 to $5. Fully label your graph.

**d** Calculate the change in quantity supplied.

2 The graph for *Dodgy Dave's* supply of DVDs drawn below is incorrect. Re-draw the graph correctly.

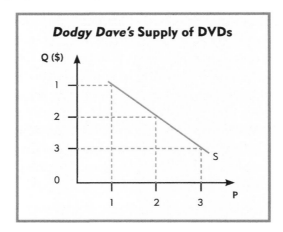

*Dodgy Dave's* **Supply of DVDs**

ISBN: 9780170193955

Economics for NCEA Level One

## Flow-on effects

An increase in the quantity supplied resulting from an increase in price is likely to mean that a firm will need to hire more staff and employ more resources in order to meet production needs.

As employment increases, households have more income to spend on goods and services, so businesses enjoy a greater demand for their products and increase their income.

Firms need to use resources other than labour, such as raw materials. An increase in demand for raw materials is likely to increase the profits of the suppliers of those materials. Any profits are then more likely to be spent within the economy, in turn providing more jobs for others.

ACTIVITY

1   Copy the terms in column A and match them with the correct definition in column B.

| Column A | Column B |
|---|---|
| **1**  supply curve | **a**  a graph showing the quantities that will be produced at a range of prices, *ceteris paribus* |
| **2**  supply schedule | **b**  as prices rise, the quantities supplied also rise, *ceteris paribus* |
| **3**  producer | **c**  a table showing the quantities that will be produced at a range of prices, *ceteris paribus* |
| **4**  supply | **d**  any individual or firm that supplies goods or services |
| **5**  Law of Supply | **e**  the quantity of a good or service that a producer is willing and able to sell at a range of prices at a certain time |

2   Pam owns and operates a business called *Soul Care*, where she goes to elderly people's homes to give pedicures and take care of their feet and toenails. The price she can charge per visit is the most important factor in determining how many hours each day she will work. At $8 per visit she would be willing to see three clients a day. At $12 per visit, she would be willing to see six clients per day. At $16 she would visit nine clients, and at $20 she would be prepared to visit 12 clients.

   **a**  Complete Pam's supply schedule for pedicures per day.
   **b**  Draw a fully labeled graph to show *Soul Care*'s supply per day.
   **c**  Fully explain what Pam is *likely to do* if the price of a pedicure was increased to $28.

ISBN: 9780170193955

# 14 ▪ Non-price internal factors affecting supply

**By the end of this unit you will be able to:**

- Describe the non-price internal factors that will affect producer choices regarding supply.
- Use the supply model to explain how a producer will react to changes in the non-price internal factors.

## Influencing supply

Other than price, there are four factors that the firm has some control over, which can affect supply. They are known as internal non-price factors affecting supply.

The four non-price internal factors affecting supply that we will investigate are:

- Costs of production
- Price of other goods the firm is able to produce (or could produce)
- Technological developments
- Productivity increases.

We are now looking at situations where something other than price changes, removing the assumption of *ceteris paribus* (that all other things will remain the same). If the costs of production change because technology or productivity improves, or if the price of another good or service that the firm can produce changes, the figures on the supply schedule are likely to change. When this happens there is a change in supply, that is, a change in the amount of a good or service that the firm is willing and able to produce.

## Costs of production

**Production costs** are the cost of inputs into the production process and may include wages, raw materials, rent and interest.

If production costs increase and selling price remains the same, then the profit margin will decrease. At this price, the producer is only willing and able to sell a smaller quantity. A new supply schedule will need to be created.

ISBN: 9780170193955

Below is *Biland's Timber Yard* supply schedule for pine framing timber.

### *Biland's Timber Yard* Monthly Supply Schedule for Pine Framing Timber

| Price ($) | Quantity supplied (000 metres) |
|-----------|-------------------------------|
| 2.00 | 100 |
| 3.00 | 150 |
| 4.00 | 200 |
| 5.00 | 250 |
| 6.00 | 300 |

If the cost of wages and rent increased, then *Biland's Timber Yard* would be unable to supply as much timber at the same price because it is costing more to produce the same amount. They will have to generate a new supply schedule:

### *Biland's Timber Yard* Monthly Supply Schedule for Pine Framing Timber

| Price ($) | Quantity supplied (000 metres) | |
|-----------|------|------|
| 2.00 | 100 | 50 |
| 3.00 | 150 | 100 |
| 4.00 | 200 | 150 |
| 5.00 | 250 | 200 |
| 6.00 | 300 | 250 |

The shift from the old supply schedule to the new one can be shown on a supply curve:

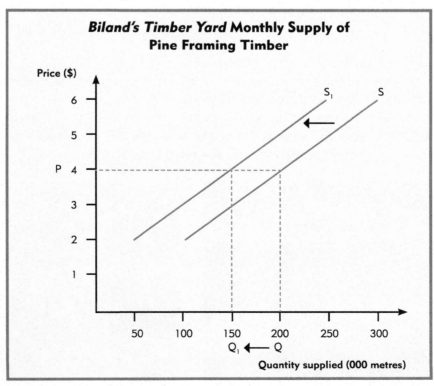

ISBN: 9780170193955

At $4 per metre, *Biland's Timber Yard* are now only willing and able to supply 150 000 metres of pine framing timber. This decrease in supply is shown by the supply curve shifting to the left. The new curve is labelled $S_1$ to show that it is a new curve. The arrows and dotted lines show that, at this price, the firm is willing and able to supply less than it did previously.

Note the differences in terminology: When there is a change in **price** there is a change in the **quantity supplied**, as shown in the supply schedule. When there is a change in a factor other than price (a **non-price** factor), there is a change in **supply**.

If there is a decrease in the production costs, then there is an increase in supply at each of those prices and the supply curve shifts to the right, because it becomes more profitable.

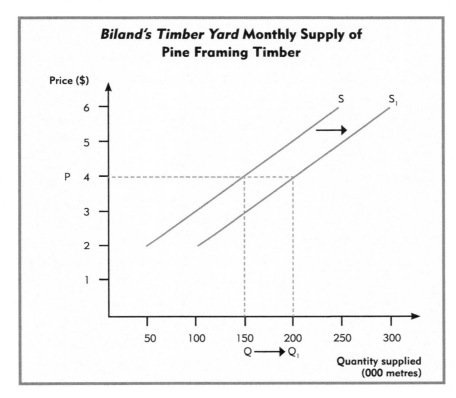

Now that the production costs have fallen, the firm is willing and able to supply more at $4. This increase in supply is shown by a shift of the supply curve to the right.

## Price of other goods

Firms can often use their resources to produce various goods and services. The price of other goods or services the firm can produce has an impact on the supply of the original product.

Let us assume that *Ruby's Ragtrade* currently supplies clothing, but is also able to produce handbags. If the price of handbags increases, then the quantity of handbags supplied will increase as the Law of Supply tells us. Ruby will switch production to handbags, decreasing the supply of clothing.

This can be shown on supply curves.

ISBN: 9780170193955

Economics for NCEA Level One

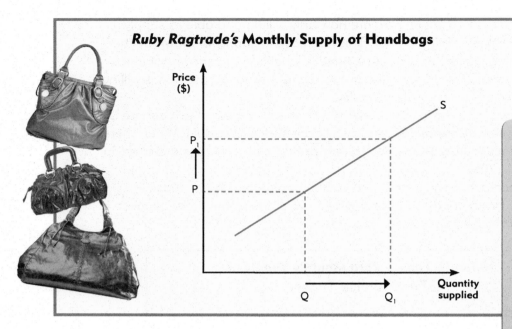

### *Ruby Ragtrade's* Monthly Supply of Handbags

As the price of handbags increases, the quantity supplied increases and there is a movement along the curve. Resources need to shift from producing clothing to producing handbags. Supplying clothing becomes relatively less profitable. This leads to a decrease in the supply of clothing and a shift of the supply curve to the left.

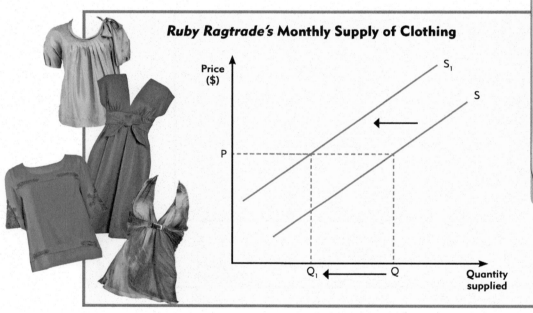

### *Ruby Ragtrade's* Monthly Supply of Clothing

## Technological developments

Advances in technology allow producers to increase their supply. Improved technology often means that production processes will be more efficient, so more output can be produced using the same input. This means that it is more cost effective to produce the good or service, and therefore more profitable to supply. A greater quantity is therefore supplied at each and every price.

On the next page is a supply curve for oranges at *Aarti's Farm*, and shows the increase in supply when she invests in new farming equipment.

ISBN: 9780170193955

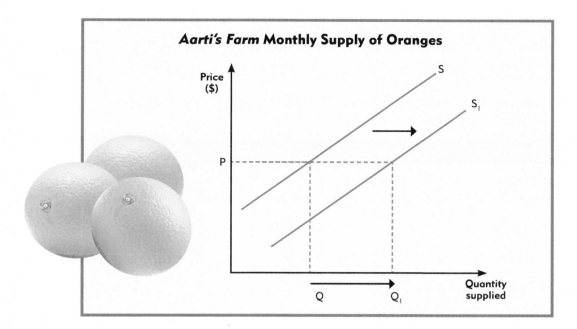

*Aarti's Farm* **Monthly Supply of Oranges**

If technology wears out or breaks down, then supply will decrease and the supply curve will shift to the left.

## Productivity increases

Productivity is output per unit of input. It is a measure of efficiency in a firm. Technology can increase productivity. Productivity can also be improved by increasing specialisation within the firm and by adopting division of labour. When there is an increase in productivity, workers will be able to produce more for the same cost, increasing the profitability of that product. Therefore supply will increase, shifting the supply curve to the right.

The graph below illustrates the change in supply as Annabelle discovers better ways of creating and packing her gift baskets for her firm *Baskets by Design*. She has been able to increase productivity, meaning she is able to produce more baskets in the same time.

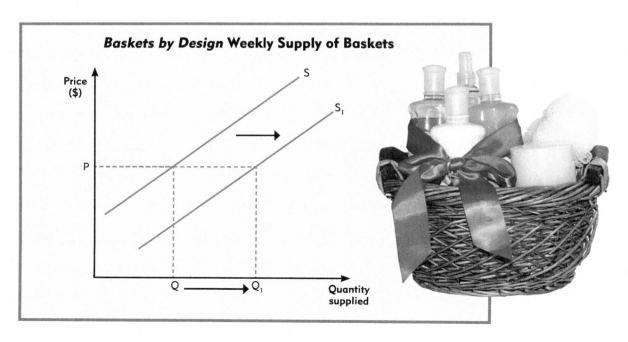

*Baskets by Design* **Weekly Supply of Baskets**

ISBN: 9780170193955

Economics for NCEA Level One

ISBN: 9780170193955

ACTIVITY

1   Use the supply model to explain the difference between the way a producer will react to a change in price compared to a change in costs.

2   Copy and complete the links in this table. One set of links has been completed as an example.

| Change | Results in | Shown as | Graph |
|---|---|---|---|
| Increase in price | Increase in supply | Movement down | |
| Increase in costs | Decrease in quantity supplied | Shift right | |
| Improved technology | Increase in quantity supplied | Shift left | |
| Decrease in price | Decrease in supply | Movement up | |

3   Give possible reasons for each of the changes shown on the graphs below.

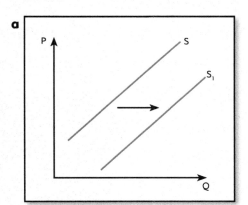

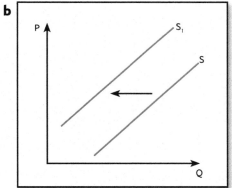

ACTIVITY

**c**

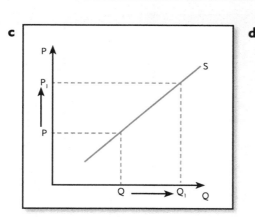

**d**

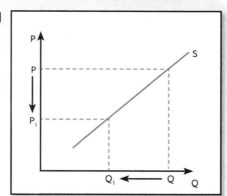

4 Copy and complete the table below. The first scenario has been done for you as an example.

| The Supply of Josie's Amazing Hot Sausages in Bread | | | |
|---|---|---|---|
| **Scenario** | **Factor** | **Graph** | **Explanation** |
| Workers wages rise | Increase in costs of production | | The increase in costs makes the business less profitable and so Josie will supply less at each price. There is a *decrease in supply*. |
| Bread falls in price | | | |
| | Improved technology | | |
| | | | This is an increase in *quantity supplied*. It is a *movement* up the supply curve. |

ISBN: 9780170193955

## The Supply of Josie's Amazing Hot Sausages in Bread (continued)

| Scenario | Factor | Graph | Explanation |
|---|---|---|---|
| | Costs of production fall | P → Q | There is an increase in *supply* as it has become more profitable. It is a *shift to the right* of the supply curve. |
| Hamburgers rise in price | | P → Q | |
| | Price of other goods we make falls | P → Q | |

**5** Finn's movie theatre can use its machine to make popcorn or caramel corn.

   **a** Use the supply model to fully explain what would happen to the supply of popcorn if the price of caramel corn increased.

   **b** Use the supply model to fully explain what would happen to the supply of popcorn if the price of caramel corn decreased.

ISBN: 9780170193955

# 15 ▪ Non-price external factors affecting supply

**By the end of this unit you will be able to:**

- Describe the non-price external factors that will affect producer choices regarding supply.
- Use the supply model to explain how a producer will react to changes in the non-price external factors affecting supply.
- Use the supply model to explain possible flow-on effects of changes in supply.

## Non-price external factors

The previous units have addressed the internal factors – factors within the firm – that affect supply. The first was price, which affects the quantity supplied and these changes were shown by a movement along the supply curve. Other factors that affect supply are **non-price factors**, and these changes result in a shift of the curve itself.

In this unit we address external non-price factors that affect supply. These factors are outside of the firm and may include things that the firm has little or no control over, such as:

- Environmental issues
- Legal requirements
- Political decisions
- Trade restrictions
- Cultural obligations.

As these are non-price factors, changes in them will *cause the supply curve to shift*.

## Environmental issues

There are two aspects of environmental issues that may affect supply.

1 Factors completely beyond the control of the business, such as acts of nature, can have a huge impact on supply. When an Icelandic volcano erupted in April 2010, for example, sending ash into the skies, air travel throughout the Northern Hemisphere came to a standstill. Planes were unable to fly because the risk of ash getting into their engines was too high, and supply of those services had to stop immediately. More than 100 000 flights were cancelled, affecting more than seven million passengers. It is estimated that the total cost of the flight disruption was more than US$4 billion.

ISBN: 9780170193955

**2** Other environmental factors concern sustainability. It may be that firms want to become more environmentally friendly, and so make choices to use their resources in a more environmentally friendly way:

- A firm may decide to use solar power, which decreases costs of production in the long term, meaning that the firm is willing and able to increase supply, producing more at that same price when it becomes more profitable to do so.
- A coal mining company restores land to its pre-mining condition (apart from the missing coal). This incurs a huge cost, which increases the costs of production, resulting in a decrease in supply.
- A trucking company may invest in tree plantations in order to offset their carbon emissions, increasing their costs of production and decreasing supply.

- A firm may decide to lower its costs of production by using more time- and energy-effective measures to lower the cost of trashing and recycling its waste, leading to an increase in supply.
- A restaurant may choose to use only organic ingredients that are more expensive. This increases the costs of production, making it less profitable to produce the same quantity at the same price. This results in a decrease in supply.

## Legal requirements

Businesses must follow the law, and what is required by the law may be outside of the firm's control. Legal requirements can have a major impact on supply:

**1** It is illegal for stores (other than those selling essential items) to open on Good Friday and Easter Sunday. If they do, and they are caught, they incur a fine. Some stores choose to open anyway. For some it is a calculated risk; firstly, hoping that they won't get caught, and secondly, that the revenue they generate will exceed the amount of the fine if they are caught. The Shop Trading Hours Act outlines how certain stores are not to be open at certain times. This is a big restriction on supply.

ISBN: 9780170193955

2   The law requires certain compliance by certain firms, such as the need to label the contents of food sold in those stores. This can mean more time in producing the good and is costly for firms, increasing the costs of production, leading to a decrease in supply.

3   There are certain legal requirements regarding production processes, for example health and safety regulations, which may increase the costs of production. Some resources will need to be used to satisfy the new standards, therefore supply decreases.

4   Staff are now entitled by law to have four weeks paid leave per year. This decreases productivity and increases the costs of production for the firm. Once again, this leads to a decrease in supply.

5   Paid parental leave entitlements introduced in the 1990s also increased costs for businesses.

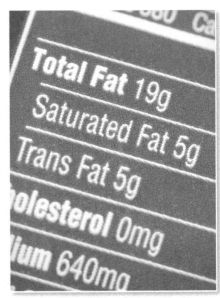

## ACTIVITY

1   Identify two other laws that might affect the supply decisions of a business.

2   Identify one law, or law change, that may increase supply.

3   Use the supply model to fully explain how producers will react to each of the scenarios above.

## Political decisions

Political factors may be imposed by a government, but differ from legal factors in that they are generated from relationships between social or philosophical viewpoints. Not everyone may agree with a given viewpoint:

- **Subsidies** are a payment given to firms by the government in order to encourage the production of a particular good or service. It may be that a firm produces a merit good, a product that society considers beneficial to you, such as safety belts or medicines. The payment given to the business represents a decrease in costs, and enables businesses to supply more at the same price. This results in more goods or services being available.

- **Sales taxes** have the opposite effect of a subsidy. A sales tax may be imposed on demerit goods, those that society considers bad for you and discourages consumption. One way a government can suppress the consumption of a demerit good is to impose a sales tax, which means that the firm must pay the government a certain percentage of their sales income. This represents an increase in costs to the business and acts to reduce supply. Through sales taxes, governments also hope the increased price of the product will discourage consumption.

- **GST (Goods and Services Tax)** is a tax imposed by the government on all goods and services sold in New Zealand (with a few exceptions). It is one way that the government earns revenue. When a government decides to

ISBN: 9780170193955

Economics for NCEA Level One

increase the rate of GST, it would increase the production costs of firms and result in decreased supply.

- Governments will sometimes restrict **trade** with other countries because they disagree with social or political events occurring within that country at the time. During apartheid in South Africa, for example, New Zealanders were not allowed to trade with South African businesses and restrictions have periodically been in force between New Zealand and countries such as Iraq, Zimbabwe and Fiji.

ACTIVITY

**1** Use the supply model to explain how the producer will react in each of the scenarios described above.

**2** Use your research skills to describe what Fair Trade Coffee is. If *Mariah's Café* has strong political feelings about the importance of supporting Fair Trade Coffee, explain how this might affect their supply decisions.

## Trade restrictions

Trading between countries normally involves a range of restrictions, usually imposed by one of the governments involved. Some countries take the view that there should be free trade, without restrictions on the goods and services exchanged between them. This increases competition and may reduce prices for consumers.

Others believe that there should be varying amounts of **protection**, which means that governments protect their local producers from the competition of overseas producers, who may be able to produce at much lower prices. There are two main forms of trade restrictions:

**1** **Quotas** are a limit on the *quantity* of goods that can be imported into a country. There is a limit on the amount of New Zealand dairy products, for example, that can be imported by countries in the European Union (a group of European countries). This protects European dairy producers from New Zealand's competitively priced dairy products. If overseas markets will only accept a certain quantity of a producers output, then the producer will limit the supply.

**2** **Tariffs** are a *tax* that governments may place on imported goods, in order to protect their local producers from too much competition. If the US government placed a 15% tariff on all its imports of New Zealand beef, then the New Zealand producer has to pay this tax, which increases the firm's production costs and leads to a decrease in supply. The tax expense will be passed onto US consumers through an increase in price, making New Zealand products less competitive and protecting American suppliers.

ISBN: 9780170193955

The **exchange rate** may also have an impact on supply. The exchange rate is the value of one currency in relation to the currency of another country. If firms are importing their raw materials, and the price of the US$ increases, for instance, then the raw materials being imported become more expensive. This increases the costs of production and will decrease supply. If the price of the overseas dollar falls, then imports become cheaper, leading to a decrease in the costs of production and an increase in supply.

**1** Use a Venn diagram to compare and contrast quotas and tariffs.

**2** Use the supply model to explain the effect of the following on supply:
 **a** A tariff on imports used in production, is lifted.
 **b** A quota on imports used in production is increased.

**3** Find out the current exchange rate for:
 **a** Aus$
 **b** US$
 **c** Euro.

## Cultural obligations

Cultural beliefs or obligations may impact on supply.

The Resource Management Act specifies that Maori culture, traditions, ancestral lands, water, sites, waahi tapu and taonga are matters of national importance that shall be 'recognised and provided for' in achieving the purpose of the Act. The Act and the Treaty of Waitangi provide for tangata whenua to be involved in decisions regarding resource management.

If a firm was to develop their business near an area close to ancestral lands, they may need to involve the tangata whenua in terms of the potential impact of the development on Maori interests.

This in itself may increase costs of production, and therefore have an impact on supply.

ISBN: 9780170193955

Economics for NCEA Level One

**Supply**

The amount of a good or service a producer is willing and able to buy at various prices at a certain time

Factors affecting supply

Price

Non-price factors

**Law of Supply**: as the price increases, the quantity supplied increases, *ceteris paribus*, vice versa

Change in price leads to a change in **quantity supplied** and a movement along the curve

Internal Non-Price Factors
- Cost of Production
- Technology developments
- Price of other goods to the firm can produce
- Productivity increases

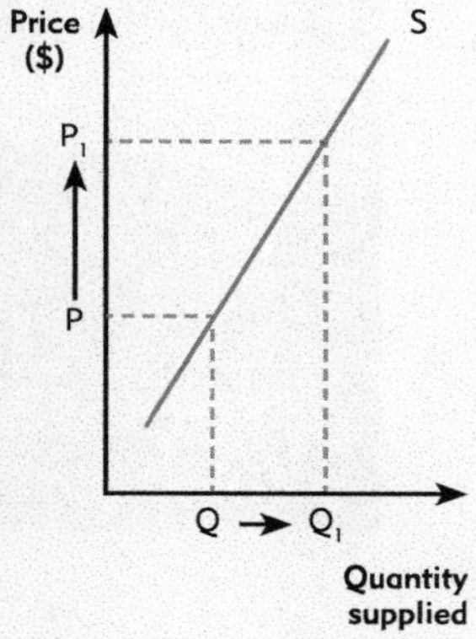

External Non-Price Factors
- Environmental Issues
- Legal requirements
- Political decisions
- Trade restrictions
- Cultural obligations

A change in a non-price factor results in a change in **supply** and a **shift** of the curve

Decrease in price, decrease in quantity supplied

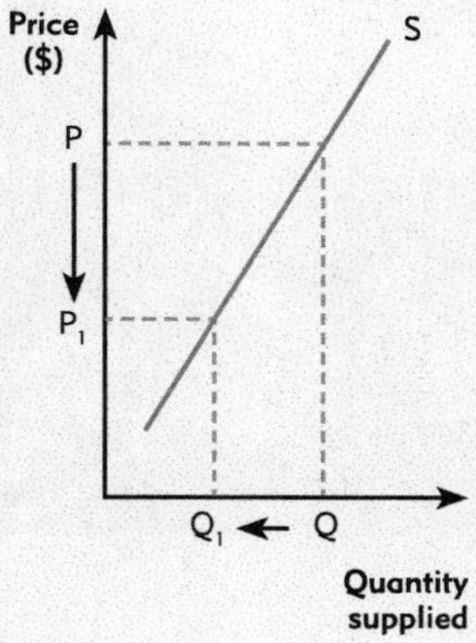

Increase in price, increase in quantity supplied

Increase in supply

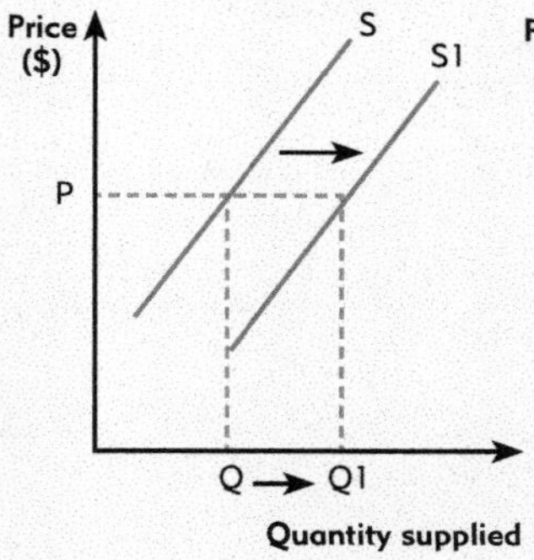

Decrease in supply

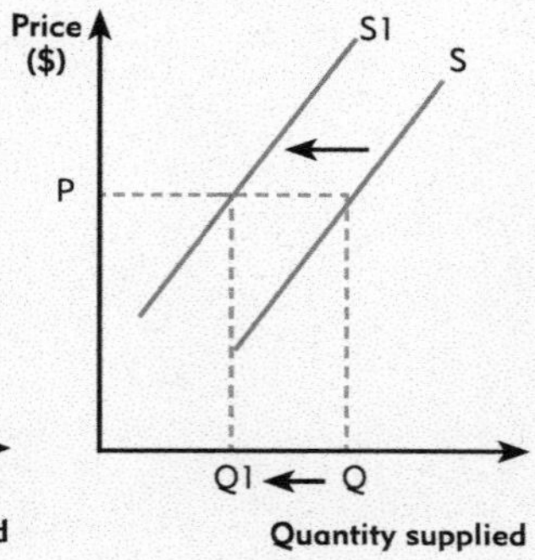

ISBN: 9780170193955

ACTIVITY

1  Use your research skills to find out what tapu means. Explain how it might affect the supply decisions of a firm.

2  Copy and complete the chart below.

| The Supply of Antonio's Awesome Sausages in Bread | | | |
|---|---|---|---|
| Scenario | Factor | Graph | Explanation |
| Sausage sizzle attendants to wear fireproof aprons | | P↑ → Q | |
| Smoke from sausage sizzles to be reduced and compulsory low smoke burners to be used | | P↑ → Q | |
| | Cultural factor | P↑ → Q | The firm needs a report from the tangata whenua before proceeding with development, increasing costs, decreasing supply, shifting the curve to the left. |
| Company taxes rise | | P↑ → Q | |
| Import taxes on US tomato ketchup removed, lower price of ketchup | | P↑ → Q | |

ISBN: 9780170193955

# Consumer, producer & government choices using supply and demand

## 16 ■ Market demand and market supply

**By the end of this unit you will be able to:**

- Define a market.
- Identify a range of markets.
- Explain that a market for a good or service is made up of all suppliers of that good or service and all of the consumers of that good or service.
- Define and derive market demand and market supply.

## Markets

A **market** is any place or situation where buyers and sellers interact to exchange goods and services. It is important to note that the buyers and sellers must be able to communicate, but they do not have to meet face to face.

## The diversity of markets

Not all markets look the same. The pictures on the next page are all markets.

**ACTIVITY**

**1** List ten different markets. Use the images on page 105 to help you.

**2** For each market you have identified, state:
  **a** Who is the buyer?
  **b** Who is the seller?
  **c** What is the product?
  **d** Is it a place or a situation?

**3** Describe what a transaction is.

ISBN: 9780170193955

**Exchange Rates**

| | | We Sell |
| --- | --- | --- |
| | AUSTRALIA | 0.8264 |
| | BRAZIL | 0.5263 |
| | CANADA | 0.9677 |
| | CHINA | 0.1417 |
| | Costa Rica | 0.00023 |
| | Euro | 1.4093 |
| | HONG KONG | 0.1412 |
| | JAPAN | 0.0094 |
| | MEXICO | 0.1014 |
| | NEW ZEALAND | 0.7284 |
| | S Korea | 0.001 |
| | SINGAPORE | 0.6982 |
| | Sweden | 0.1508 |
| | Switzerland | 0.8837 |
| | TAHITI | 0.0123 |
| | TAIWAN | 0.0342 |
| | THAILAND | 0.0303 |
| | UNITED KIN... | |

FOR SALE

GARAGE SALE

ISBN: 9780170193955

# How does a shop differ from a market?

Markets refer to all sellers and all buyers of a particular good or service. There are specific markets, for example:

- The market for mobile phones – all the buyers of mobile phones AND all the sellers of mobile phones.
- The market for apples – all the buyers of apples AND all the sellers of apples.

There are also markets for different types of goods and services, for example:

- The market for electronic equipment – all the buyers of electronic equipment AND all the sellers of electronic equipment.
- The market for fruit and vegetables - all the buyers of fruit and vegetables AND all the sellers of fruit and vegetables.

Shops are individual sellers of a good or service. *Dick Smith*, for example, is one of the sellers in the market for electronic goods. They are part of the market but they are not the only seller. The market is made up of ALL the sellers and ALL of the buyers of a good or service.

**ACTIVITY**

1 Identify a possible market for each of these businesses: *Countdown, Hoyts Cinemas, Tuckers Panelbeaters, PioPio Plumbers, Sony, Slingshot.*

2 Assess these three students' definitions of a market and answer the questions that follow.

**Sophie**

A market is where buyers and sellers meet to exchange goods or services.

**Fergus**

A market is a place where buyers and sellers can communicate and exchange goods and services.

**Coco**

A market is a place or situation where goods and services are exchanged.

**a** Identify the best answer.
**b** Explain what this answer has that the other answers do not have.
**c** Are there any other details that this student could have included?

ISBN: 9780170193955

Consumer, producer & government choices using supply and demand

We can use our knowledge of supply and demand to illustrate what happens in a market when buyers and sellers interact.

> **Demand** is the quantity of a good or service that a consumer is willing and able to buy at a range of prices at a certain time.
>
> **Supply** is the quantity of a good or service that a producer is willing and able to sell at a range of prices at a certain time.

In referring to a market we are including *all* of the producers who supply that market and *all* of the consumers who demand the goods or services in that market.

- **Market demand** is the quantity of a good or service that *all* consumers are willing and able to buy at different prices.
- **Market supply** is the quantity of a good or service that *all* producers are willing and able to sell at different prices.

**ACTIVITY**

1 Distinguish between individual supply and market supply.

2 Distinguish between individual demand and market demand.

We can show market demand and market supply in a table and on a graph just as we did for individual demand and supply (see Units 2 and 13).

## Market demand

The market demand is found by the **horizontal summation** of the individual demand curves, or demand schedules.

Market demand measures the demand of all consumers for a product. This could mean everyone globally, nationally, in your neighbourhood or at a particular event, depending on where the product is available.

ISBN: 9780170193955

Economics for NCEA Level One

# The lemonade stand

Let us consider the market demand for homemade lemonade for sale in Lucy's front yard. There are three people who are willing and able to buy lemonade: Dad, Nana and Lucy's big brother Darius. (Baby Noni is willing to buy it but has no money, so cannot be included in our market demand.)

The individual demand schedules and demand curves for Dad, Nana and Darius are shown below:

| Dad's Daily Demand Schedule for Homemade Lemonade | |
|---|---|
| Price ($) | Quantity (glasses) |
| 1 | 3 |
| 2 | 2 |
| 3 | 1 |

| Nana's Daily Demand Schedule for Homemade Lemonade | |
|---|---|
| Price ($) | Quantity (glasses) |
| 1 | 4 |
| 2 | 3 |
| 3 | 2 |

| Darius' Daily Demand Schedule for Homemade Lemonade | |
|---|---|
| Price ($) | Quantity (glasses) |
| 1 | 2 |
| 2 | 1 |
| 3 | 0 |

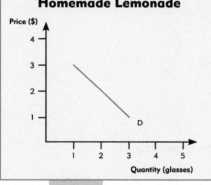

**Dad's Daily Demand for Homemade Lemonade**

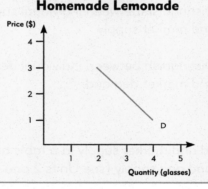

**Nana's Daily Demand for Homemade Lemonade**

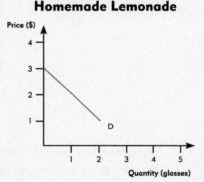

**Darius's Daily Demand for Homemade Lemonade**

How do we explain the information taken from these tables and graphs?

Dad will demand:
- 3 glasses a day when the price is $1
- 2 glasses a day when the price is $2
- 1 glasses a day when the price is $3

Nana will demand:
- 4 glasses a day when the price is $1
- 3 glasses a day when the price is $2
- 2 glasses a day when the price is $3

Darius will demand:
- 2 glasses a day when the price is $1
- 1 glasses a day when the price is $2
- 0 glasses a day when the price is $3

ISBN: 9780170193955

Consumer, producer & government choices using supply and demand

In total, therefore, if the price is $1 the market (all buyers: Dad, Nana and Darius) will demand:

3 + 4 + 2 = 9 glasses of lemonade per day.

If the price is $2 the market (all buyers: Dad, Nana and Darius) will demand:

2 + 3 + 1 = 6 glasses of lemonade per day.

If the price is $3 the market (all buyers: Dad, Nana and Darius) will demand:

1 + 2 + 0 = 3 glasses of lemonade per day.

We can use this information to create a **Market Demand Schedule**.

| The Daily Market Demand Schedule for Homemade Lemonade | |
|---|---|
| Price ($) | Quantity (glasses) |
| 1 | 9 |
| 2 | 6 |
| 3 | 3 |

From this table we can plot a **Market Demand Curve**.

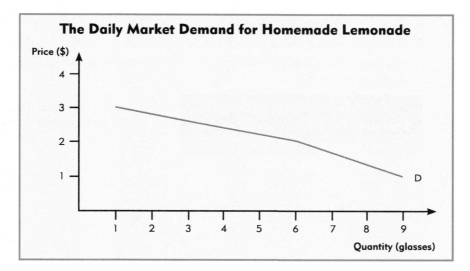

The Daily Market Demand for Homemade Lemonade

1 Using the case study above:
   **a** Explain why the market demand curve is the horizontal summation of individual demand curves.
   **b** Explain why prices have remained the same in the market demand curve as they were in the individual demand curves.

2 The following set of individual demand schedules represents the entire market demand for mixed lollies. Graph the market demand curve for mixed lollies.

ISBN: 9780170193955

| Emelia's Annual Demand Schedule for Bags of Mixed Lollies | |
|---|---|
| Price ($) | Quantity (00) |
| 0.50 | 10 |
| 0.60 | 8 |
| 0.70 | 6 |
| 0.80 | 4 |
| 0.90 | 2 |
| 1.00 | 1 |

| Niamh's Annual Demand Schedule for Bags of Mixed Lollies | |
|---|---|
| Price ($) | Quantity (00) |
| 0.50 | 12 |
| 0.60 | 11 |
| 0.70 | 10 |
| 0.80 | 9 |
| 0.90 | 8 |
| 1.00 | 7 |

| Harry's Annual Demand Schedule for Bags of Mixed Lollies | |
|---|---|
| Price ($) | Quantity (00) |
| 0.50 | 6 |
| 0.60 | 5 |
| 0.70 | 4 |
| 0.80 | 3 |
| 0.90 | 2 |
| 1.00 | 1 |

**3** The following individual demands represent the entire market demand for gymnastic lessons. Graph the market demand curve for gymnastic lessons per year.

| Danielle's Annual Demand Schedule for Gymnastics Lessons | |
|---|---|
| Price ($/hour) | Quantity (hours) |
| 25.00 | 70 |
| 22.50 | 75 |
| 20.00 | 80 |
| 17.50 | 85 |
| 15.00 | 90 |
| 12.50 | 95 |
| 10.00 | 100 |

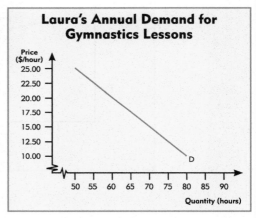

Laura's Annual Demand for Gymnastics Lessons

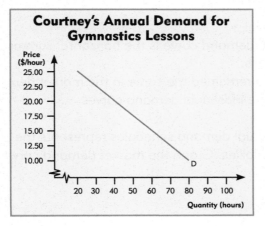

Courtney's Annual Demand for Gymnastics Lessons

A large empty space on a graph is a waste of space and is *not acceptable* when presenting information. Either adjust the scale of your axis, or add a break on the axis of your graph to show you are not starting at zero.

ISBN: 9780170193955

Consumer, producer & government choices using supply and demand

# Market supply

We can find market supply in much the same way that we found market demand. Let us look at the supply of slushies in Ashburton, assuming that there are only three suppliers. Here are their supply schedules and supply curves:

| *Slushman's* Daily Supply Schedule for Slushies | |
|---|---|
| Price ($) | Quantity (per day) |
| 1 | 40 |
| 2 | 120 |
| 3 | 160 |

| *Slushmaestro's* Daily Supply Schedule for Slushies | |
|---|---|
| Price ($) | Quantity (per day) |
| 1 | 60 |
| 2 | 140 |
| 3 | 160 |

| *Slush is Us'* Daily Supply Schedule for Slushies | |
|---|---|
| Price ($) | Quantity (per day) |
| 1 | 100 |
| 2 | 120 |
| 3 | 140 |

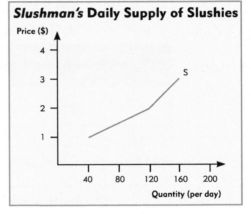

**Slushman's** Daily Supply of Slushies

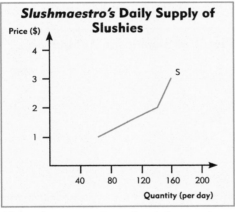

**Slushmaestro's** Daily Supply of Slushies

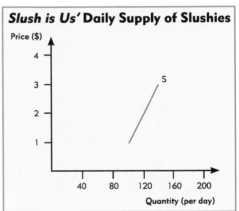

**Slush is Us'** Daily Supply of Slushies

How do we explain the information taken from these tables and graphs?

*Slushman* will supply:
- 40 slushies a day when the price is $1
- 120 slushies a day when the price is $2
- 160 slushies a day when the price is $3

*Slushmaestro* will supply:
- 60 slushies a day when the price is $1
- 140 slushies a day when the price is $2
- 160 slushies a day when the price is $3

ISBN: 9780170193955

Economics for NCEA Level One

*Slush is Us* will supply:

- 100 slushies a day when the price is $1
- 120 slushies a day when the price is $2
- 140 slushies a day when the price is $3

In total, therefore, if the price is $1 the market (all suppliers: *Slushman*, *Slushmaestro* and *Slush is Us*) will supply:

> 40 + 60 + 100 = 200 slushies per day.

If the price is $2 the market (all suppliers: *Slushman*, *Slushmaestro* and *Slush is Us*) will supply:

> 120 + 140 + 120 = 380 slushies per day.

If the price is $3 the market (all suppliers: *Slushman*, *Slushmaestro* and *Slush is Us*) will supply:

> 160 + 160 + 140= 460 slushies per day.

We can use this information to create a market supply schedule.

| The Daily Market Supply Schedule for Slushies in Ashburton | |
|---|---|
| Price ($) | Quantity (per day) |
| 1 | 200 |
| 2 | 380 |
| 3 | 400 |

And from this schedule we can plot a market supply curve.

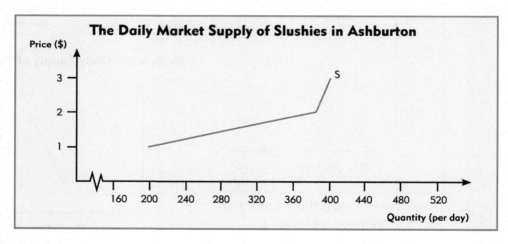

The Daily Market Supply of Slushies in Ashburton

1 Using the case study above:
   a Explain why the market supply curve is the horizontal summation of individual supply curves.
   b Explain why prices have remained the same in the market supply curve as they were in the individual supply curves

ISBN: 9780170193955

Consumer, producer & government choices using supply and demand

ISBN: 9780170193955

**2** Use the following individual supply schedules to create a market supply schedule and market supply curve for lollipops.

| Cory's Corner Dairy Weekly Supply Schedule for Lollipops | |
|---|---|
| Price ($) | Quantity (boxes) |
| 4 | 9 |
| 6 | 12 |
| 8 | 15 |

| Mitzi's Mid-Street Dairy Weekly Supply Schedule for Lollipops | |
|---|---|
| Price ($) | Quantity (boxes) |
| 4 | 18 |
| 6 | 20 |
| 8 | 26 |

| Dinesh's Downtown Dairy Weekly Supply Schedule for Lollipops | |
|---|---|
| Price ($) | Quantity (boxes) |
| 4 | 8 |
| 6 | 11 |
| 8 | 19 |

**3** Use the following individual supply curves to create a market supply schedule and market supply curve for eggs.

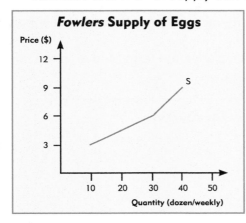

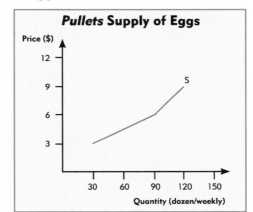

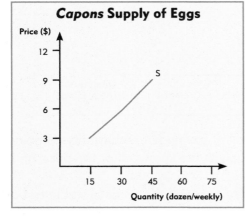

**4** Compare the market demand for lollypops in question **2** and the market supply for eggs in question **3**. Outline how the time frame can be shown in a demand schedule or a demand curve.

Economics for NCEA Level One

# 17 ▪ Market equilibrium

**By the end of this unit you will be able to:**

- Illustrate the market using the Supply and Demand Model.
- Illustrate and define market equilibrium.
- Explain and illustrate excess supply and excess demand.
- Fully explain how market forces work to bring the market into equilibrium.

## Market demand

A market is any place or situation where buyers and sellers can communicate and exchange goods or services.

The most familiar form of market is the retail market, which includes all retail outlets, typically called shops. Modern technology has changed the style of markets and Internet shops exist in cyberspace and are also part of the retail market.

We can represent the market using the Supply and Demand Model. We use the market demand curve to indicate all buyers, and the market supply curve to indicate all sellers.

The graph of this model always includes the term Market in the title, indicating that *both* demand and supply are shown.

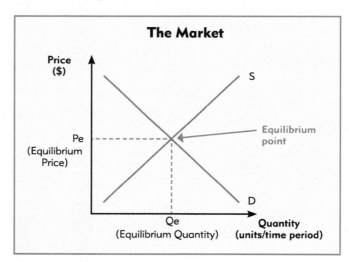

The market demand curve shows all of the price and quantity combinations that satisfy consumers. The market supply curve shows all of the price and quantity combinations that satisfy producers.

There is only one point on the entire graph that is acceptable to *both* consumers and producers. This point is the **equilibrium point**. The word equilibrium means stable, and therefore the equilibrium point of a market is a stable point in the market.

The equilibrium point gives us the **equilibrium price** and **equilibrium quantity** combination that is acceptable to both producers and consumers. Price equilibrium and quantity equilibrium are commonly labelled Pe and Qe but other labels are acceptable.

ISBN: 9780170193955

To explain why the equilibrium is stable, economists usually start by explaining what happens when the market is not at equilibrium. The market is NOT at equilibrium when the price is higher than the equilibrium price, nor when the price is lower than the equilibrium price.

## Prices higher than equilibrium

At any price higher than Pe, the quantity demanded is lower than the quantity supplied. On the graph below this is shown as $P_1$.

There is a **surplus** in the market. This is also called **excess supply**.

Producers have unsold goods and services, so they lower their prices to try to sell them.

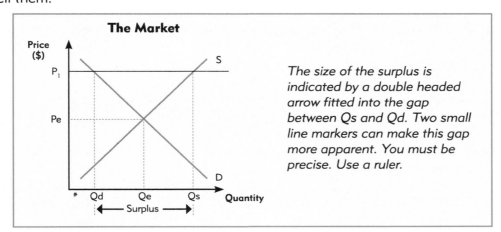

*The size of the surplus is indicated by a double headed arrow fitted into the gap between Qs and Qd. Two small line markers can make this gap more apparent. You must be precise. Use a ruler.*

As the price is lowered, the laws of supply and demand tell us that the quantity supplied will decrease and the quantity demanded will increase *until* the point where the quantity supplied equals the quantity demanded. This point is the equilibrium.

There is no longer any reason for producers to continue to drop their prices, so once the market reaches the equilibrium price it will stay there – in other words, the market is stable. There is no surplus anymore and the market has **cleared**.

## Prices lower than equilibrium

At any price lower than Pe, the quantity demanded is higher than the quantity supplied. On the graph below this is shown as $P_2$.

There is a **shortage** in the market. This is also called an **excess demand**.

Consumers cannot get the good or service they are willing and able to buy. They bid the price up to make sure they can get it. (This is what happens at an auction; it is consumers who are making the prices go up!)

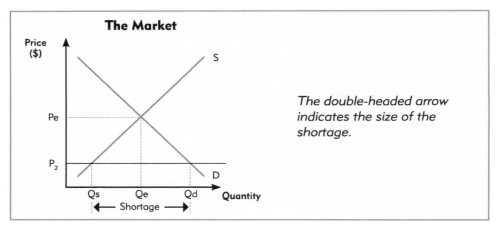

*The double-headed arrow indicates the size of the shortage.*

Consumer, producer & government choices using supply and demand

ISBN: 9780170193955

Economics for NCEA Level One

ISBN: 9780170193955

As the price rises the laws of demand and supply tell us that the quantity demanded will decrease and the quantity supplied will increase *until* the quantity demanded equals the quantity supplied. This point is the equilibrium.

There is no longer any reason for consumers to continue to bid prices up, so once the equilibrium price is reached it will stay there and the market is stable. There is no longer any shortage and the market has cleared.

Pressure on the market comes from the need of consumers for goods and services and the need of producers to sell their goods and services. These pressures are known as **market forces** or 'the invisible hand'.

Markets will always be at equilibrium *or* on their way to equilibrium. Once at equilibrium the pressures are gone and the market is stable.

ACTIVITY

**1** Explain how a market reacts to a shortage.

**2** Explain how a market responds to a surplus.

**3** Use *TradeMe* as an example to explain why consumers raise prices when they want to buy things as cheaply as possible.

**4** Explain why a producer would lower prices when they can make larger profits at higher prices.

**5** Plot the following figures accurately on a graph and derive the market price, then answer the questions that follow. Ensure your diagram is fully labelled and clearly identify equilibrium price (Pe) and equilibrium quantity (Qe).

| | Market for Milk | |
|---|---|---|
| Price ($/litre) | Quantity demanded (million litres) | Quantity supplied (million litres) |
| 3.95 | 75 | 15 |
| 3.96 | 70 | 20 |
| 3.97 | 65 | 25 |
| 3.98 | 60 | 30 |
| 3.99 | 55 | 35 |
| 4.00 | 50 | 40 |
| 4.01 | 45 | 45 |
| 4.02 | 40 | 50 |
| 4.03 | 35 | 60 |
| 4.04 | 30 | 65 |
| 4.05 | 25 | 70 |
| 4.06 | 20 | 75 |
| 4.07 | 15 | 80 |

**a** Describe the situation that would arise if the suppliers made an error and charged a price *above* the equilibrium price you have derived. Show this on your graph and explain in words the sequence of events that would follow.

**b** If the price of milk was set *below* your market price, describe the situation that would arise. Explain in words the sequence of events that would follow.

ACTIVITY

**6** Copy the terms in column A and match them with the correct definition in column B.

| Column A | Column B |
|---|---|
| **1** equilibrium price | **a** the graph that shows the quantities that will be produced at a range of prices, *ceteris paribus* |
| **2** non-equilibrium prices | **b** an excess of demand |
| **3** shortage | **c** the providers of goods and services |
| **4** surplus | **d** prices where there is pressure to change |
| **5** market forces | **e** pressure within the market to move to the equilibrium point |
| **6** consumers | **f** an excess of supply |
| **7** producers | **g** a table that shows the quantities that will be bought at a range of prices, *ceteris paribus* |
| **8** demand schedule | **h** the price at which the quantity supplied equals the quantity demanded |
| **9** supply curve | **i** the users of goods and services |

**7** Plot the market diagram from the schedules below and answer the questions that follow. Clearly identify equilibrium price (Pe) and equilibrium quantity (Qe) on your graph.

| Market Demand Schedule for Apricots | | Market Supply Schedule for Apricots | |
|---|---|---|---|
| **Price ($)** | **Quantity (000 kg)** | **Price ($)** | **Quantity (000 kg)** |
| 1.00 | 18 | 1.00 | 10 |
| 1.10 | 17 | 1.10 | 11 |
| 1.20 | 16 | 1.20 | 12 |
| 1.30 | 15 | 1.30 | 13 |
| 1.40 | 14 | 1.40 | 14 |
| 1.50 | 13 | 1.50 | 15 |
| 1.30 | 12 | 1.30 | 16 |
| 1.70 | 11 | 1.70 | 17 |

**a** Explain what would happen if the producers decided to sell their apricots at $1.10/kg.

**b** Explain what would happen if producers decided to sell their apricots at $1.70/kg.

**c** Using your answers to the previous two questions, explain why the market will eventually operate at $1.40/kg.

Consumer, producer & government choices using supply and demand

ISBN: 9780170193955

# 18 ▪ Consumer choices and market equilibrium

**By the end of this unit you will be able to:**

- Identify consumer choices that affect the market.
- Illustrate and explain the direct effect of consumer choices on the market using the Supply and Demand Model.

Although the market equilibrium can be described as stable, it is not *fixed*. This means that while equilibrium is generally unchanging this does not mean it can never change. While there is no pressure on the market to change it will remain stable. Consumers can make decisions that alter the market conditions.

Think back to the unit where the words *ceteris paribus* are first introduced. This phrase means all other factors remain the same, in other words, nothing else has changed. What happens when something does change? Consumers can make different choices and this will change the market.

## Consumer choice

You know that the buying decisions of consumers are affected by many different things, for example, what your friends are doing, the price of competing goods and services, the weather, what bands are playing this weekend, how well local sports teams are doing, what is new or what is no longer cool and can you afford it anyway?

In earlier units the non-price factors that affect your choices were put into groups. These groups are:

- Changes in the price of complementary goods
- Changes in the price of substitute goods
- Changes in income
- Changes in tastes and preferences.

Changes in any of these factors will affect your choices and impact on the market through your buying decisions.

The Supply and Demand Model can illustrate the impact of your consumer choices on the market. Some of this should be familiar from the work you did in Unit 3, the only difference is that we are looking at a market graph with demand *and* supply curves on it rather than only a demand curve or only a supply curve. This means we must also consider the impact on the equilibrium point. We need to look at the impact on equilibrium price and equilibrium quantity.

ISBN: 9780170193955

## Changes in tastes and preferences

Imagine the current market for New Zealand roast lamb:

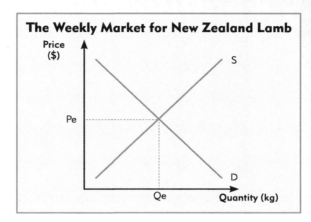

Then a nationally recognised figure fronts a series of television commercials promoting the benefits of eating lamb. Associating a famous or popular person with a product raises the demand for it. This affects our tastes and preferences; basically we like roast lamb more now because we like that particular famous person and they are recommending roast lamb.

Our increased demand for roast lamb is shown as a shift of the demand curve to the right.

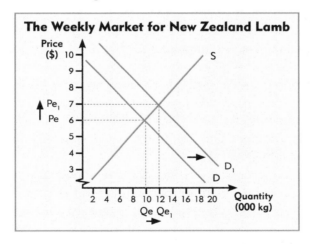

The shift has the effect of changing the equilibrium. The equilibrium price has risen from $6 to $7 per kilogram, and the equilibrium quantity has increased from 10 000 kg to 12 000 kg per week.

If price remained at $6 after demand shifted from D to $D_1$, there would be a shortage. Consumers would bid the price up until the new equilibrium was reached and the market was cleared.

Suppose the same famous person mentioned earlier then becomes highly critical of farming methods used in modern lamb farming. This will decrease our demand for roast lamb, shown as a *shift of the demand curve to the left.*

ISBN: 9780170193955

Economics for NCEA Level One

ISBN: 9780170193955

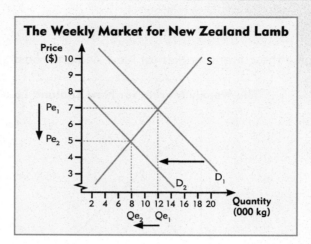

**The Weekly Market for New Zealand Lamb**

This has the effect of changing the equilibrium. The equilibrium price has fallen from $7 to $5 per kilogram. The equilibrium quantity has also decreased from 12 000 kg to 8 000 kg per week. If price remained at $7, there would be a surplus. Producers would lower their prices until equilibrium was reached and the market cleared.

Note how the change in equilibrium price and quantity is shown using labels and arrows.

## SKILLS

## Labelling and arrows

Showing changes on a supply and demand graph requires care. In the previous examples, the original equilibrium was labelled Pe and Qe. Labelling the new equilibrium *must* follow a consistent labelling style.

Our graph uses $Pe_1$ and $Qe_1$ to show the new equilibrium. The old and new style matches, in other words, they are both Pe and Qe with the small number indicating the new one. In addition, each pair matches: Pe matches Qe and $Pe_1$ matches $Qe_1$. (Note that the following pairs do *not* match: Pe with $E_q$, Pe with Q1.)

In addition to correctly using labels to show a change, the change in demand is shown by an arrow pointing in the correct direction of the change. Arrows that are used to represent the changes need to be drawn precisely. They show the direction of the change, so double-headed arrows should *not* be used.

Arrows should start at the old equilibrium point and end at the new point, and *not* go beyond those points. The arrow indicating a shift in demand or supply is drawn horizontal and in the correct direction. One arrow is enough. Try to keep arrows perfectly horizontal (for Q) or perfectly vertical (for P).

Dotted lines help make reading the graph easier by linking labels and data on the axis to key points.

## A rise in income

The government has promised a cut in personal income tax rates (PAYE), which will result in increased disposable income for households. This will increase our demand for normal goods. Eggs are an example of a normal good.

A rise in disposable income will increase our demand for eggs, shown as a shift to the right of the demand curve.

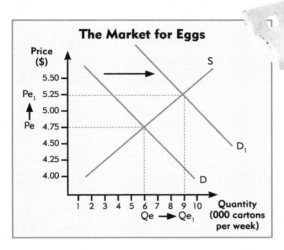

This has the effect of changing the equilibrium. The equilibrium price rose from $4.75 to $5.25 a carton. The equilibrium quantity has also risen from 6 000 to 9 000 cartons per week.

## A fall in income

Following the global financial crisis many New Zealand workers lost their jobs. Household incomes fell. This decreased our demand for normal goods. Movie tickets are an example of a normal good.

A fall in income will decrease our demand for movie tickets, shown as a shift to the left of the demand curve.

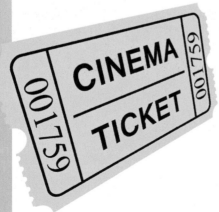

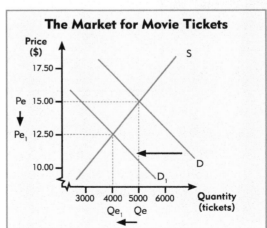

This has the effect of changing the equilibrium. The equilibrium price fell from $15.00 to $12.50 a ticket. The equilibrium quantity has also fallen from 5 000 to 4 000 tickets per week.

ISBN: 9780170193955

Economics for NCEA Level One

**ACTIVITY**

**1** Use the Supply and Demand Model to show the effect of:
  **a** A decrease in income on chuck steak (an inferior good).
  **b** An increase in income on supermarket brand cereals (an inferior good).

**2** Use the Supply and Demand Model to show the effect of:
  **a** The market for ice blocks as the weather gets colder.
  **b** The market for quiche after it is found that eggs are the new superfood.

**3** Use the Supply and Demand Model to show the effect of:
  **a** The market for netball shoes in winter.
  **b** The release of a huge new teen movie on the sale of movie-related merchandise.

**CASE STUDY**

## Changes in the price of complementary goods

MP3 players and online music are examples of complementary goods. Online music companies are lowering the price of each track to try to increase the legitimate sale of music online.

This will increase the quantity demanded of online music tracks. It also means the demand for MP3 players will increase as consumers need somewhere to play their music tracks. This is shown as a shift to the right of the demand curve for MP3 players.

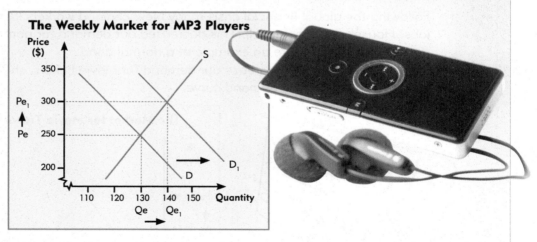

**The Weekly Market for MP3 Players**

This has the effect of changing the equilibrium. The equilibrium price has risen from $250 to $300. The equilibrium quantity has also risen from 130 per week to 140 per week.

Consumer, producer & government choices using supply and demand

## CASE STUDY

# Changes in the price of substitute goods

Pizza and hamburgers are examples of substitute goods. Pizza sellers are lowering their prices to try to increase sales. This will increase the quantity demanded of pizza. It also means that although the price of hamburgers has not changed, consumers will buy fewer hamburgers because they are now buying (and eating!) pizza. This is shown as a shift to the left of the demand curve for hamburgers.

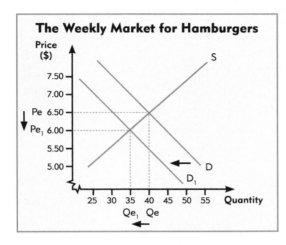

**The Weekly Market for Hamburgers**

This has the effect of changing the equilibrium. The equilibrium price fell from $6.50 to $6.00 per hamburger. The equilibrium quantity has fallen from 40 000 to 35 000 per week.

## ACTIVITY

1 Copy and complete the following chart:

| The Market for Pies | | | |
|---|---|---|---|
| **Scenario** | **Factor** | **Graph** | **Explanation** |
| Traditional Kiwi food becomes the next big food fad | Taste and preferences have moved toward the product | [graph showing S, $P_2$, $P_1$, $D_1$, $D_2$, $Q_1 \rightarrow Q_2$] | This is an increase in **demand**<br>The equilibrium **price** will rise<br>The equilibrium **quantity** will rise |
| Tomato sauce falls in price | | [blank P/Q axes] | |
| Huge obesity awareness campaign blames New Zealanders weight problems on our love of pies | | [blank P/Q axes] | |

ISBN: 9780170193955

Economics for NCEA Level One

| Scenario | Factor | Graph | Explanation |
|---|---|---|---|
| Pies are an inferior good. Household incomes fall in a period of rising unemployment | | P ↑     → Q | |
| | Price of a substitute good or service rises | P ↑     → Q | |

# 19 ▪ Producer choices and market equilibrium

**By the end of this unit you will be able to:**

- Identify producer choices that affect the market.
- Illustrate and explain the direct effect of producer choices on the market using the Supply and Demand Model.

Producer choices impact on the market and affect the equilibrium price and quantity, just as consumer choices do.

Producers are, most commonly, trying to maximise profits. The way to do this is to maximise revenue while minimising costs. Producers can change the types of resources or inputs they use, or try different methods to improve their sales and revenue. Different rules and regulations may change how certain producers operate. The state of the economy can affect the choices a producer makes in their business.

In Units 14 and 15 the influences on producer choices were classified into two groups. The first was *internal* non-price factors affecting supply:

- Changes in the price of other goods that the producer could supply
- Changes in production costs
- Changes in technology
- Changes in productivity.

The second group was *external* non-price factors affecting supply:

- Trade restrictions
- Legal requirements
- Environmental issues
- Political issues
- Cultural obligations.

Changes in any of these factors will affect producer choices and impact on the market through supply. The Supply and Demand Model can be used to illustrate this.

ISBN: 9780170193955

Consumer, producer & government choices using supply and demand

ACTIVITY

Copy the table below and sort the following factors under the correct heading:

| Factors Affecting Producer Choices | | | | | | | | |
|---|---|---|---|---|---|---|---|---|
| Changes in the price of other goods | Changes in costs of production | Changes in technology | Changes in productivity | Trade | Legal | Environment | Political | Cultural obligations |
| | | | | | | | | |

**a** Zoning laws are eased to allow more production in an area.
**b** Fall in price of raw materials.
**c** Workers wages rise.
**d** Company tax rates rise.
**e** New Zealand's emission trading scheme likely to reduce profit margins.
**f** Mining made legal in national parks.
**g** New nano-technology revolutionises manufacturing processes.
**h** Free trade agreement signed with China.
**i** Apples from Australia banned as fears of new super fruit fly grow.
**j** Increases to ACC levies announced.
**k** Least waste production methods reduce waste disposal costs.
**l** Sheep farmers notice the price of goats carcasses have increased.
**m** Iwi tighten up regarding Resource Management Act considerations.

CASE STUDY

## Increase in costs of production

Following the invasion of Iraq in 2003, the price of oil rose sharply. Oil is a key input into the plastics industry. A rise in the price of oil caused the costs of production for plastic manufacturers to rise.

This is shown as a shift of the supply curve to the left.

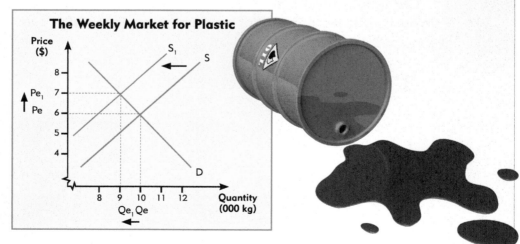

This has the effect of changing the equilibrium. The equilibrium price has risen from $6 to $7 per kilogram. The equilibrium quantity has fallen from 10 000 to 9 000 kg per week.

It is important to pay attention to labelling changes on these graphs. (Refer to page 120.)

ISBN: 9780170193955

ISBN: 9780170193955

## Decrease in costs of production

The price of the New Zealand dollar rose over a certain period. This has the effect of making imports less expensive. Imported clothing sold in retail clothing shops around the country has been cheaper to import as a result of the rise in the New Zealand dollar.

This will increase the supply of imported clothing in the retail clothing market, shown as a shift of the supply curve to the right.

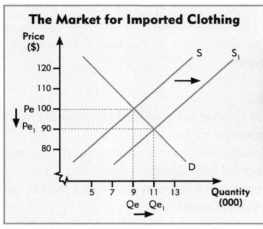

This has the effect of changing the equilibrium. The equilibrium price has fallen from $100 to $90, where the market has cleared. The equilibrium quantity has risen from 9 000 to 11 000 items of imported clothing per week.

## Legal factors

The government has strengthened safety requirements for petrol stations underground storage tanks, as a result many of the tanks will need to be replaced.

Changing production to meet these regulations will increase costs of production, shown as a shift of the supply curve to the left.

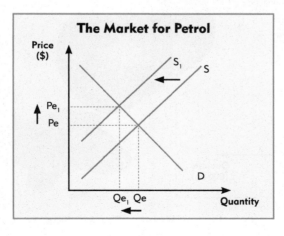

This has the effect of changing the equilibrium. The equilibrium price has risen and the equilibrium quantity has fallen.

Consumer, producer & government choices using supply and demand

**ACTIVITY**

**1** Copy and complete the following chart concerning a firm that produces paper:

| Scenario | Factor | Graph | Explanation |
|---|---|---|---|
| Cost of wood chip falls (used to make paper) | Wood chip is an input into the paper making process. This is a decrease in cost of production | P, S, S₁, Pe, Pe₁, Qe, Qe₁, Q | This is an increase in **supply**. The equilibrium **price** will **decrease**. The equilibrium **quantity** will rise. |
| Compressed wood pulp logs (something you could make instead of paper) rise in price | | P, Q | |
| New pulp making machines speed up paper making process | | P, Q | |
| Firms face fines for toxic waste spill | | P, Q | |
| | Change in legal factor | P, Q | This is an increase in supply... |

ISBN: 9780170193955

**2** Copy and complete the following chart concerning the market for banana milkshakes.

| Scenario | Graph | Explanation |
|---|---|---|
| The price of milkshake flavourings rise | <br>P<br><br>$S_1$  S<br><br>$Pe_1$<br>Pe<br><br>D<br><br>Q<br>$Qe_1$ Qe | Milkshake flavourings are an example of the costs of production. If costs of production rise then the supply decreases *(shifts to the left)*. This causes the equilibrium price to rise and the equilibrium quantity to fall. |
| The price of milkshake paper cups falls | P<br><br><br><br>Q | |
| A new improved milkshake making machine is available on the market | P<br><br><br><br>Q | |
| Import quotas on milkshake thickenings are imposed | P<br><br><br><br>Q | |
| New hygiene laws insist all handlers of milk products wear gloves | P<br><br><br><br>Q | |
| The price of smoothies rises. Milkshake producers have the resources to produce smoothies. | P<br><br><br><br>Q | |

ISBN: 9780170193955

**3** Copy and complete the chart below. You will need to identify whether it is a supply factor or a demand factor that is affected.

| The Product is Doughnuts | | | |
|---|---|---|---|
| **Scenario** | **Factor** | **Graph** | **Explanation** |
| Doughnuts are discovered to be a health food | Demand, because tastes and preferences move toward doughnuts | 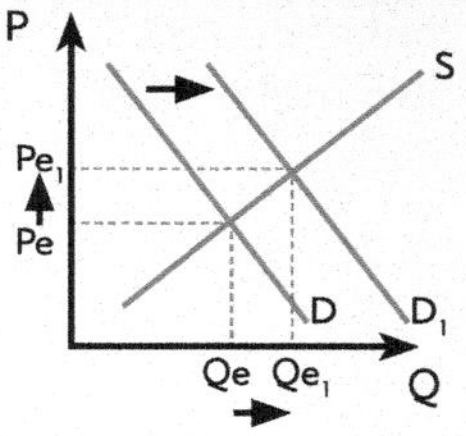 | This is an increase in demand. The equilibrium price will rise. The equilibrium quantity will rise. |
| Sugar for coating doughnuts falls in price | | 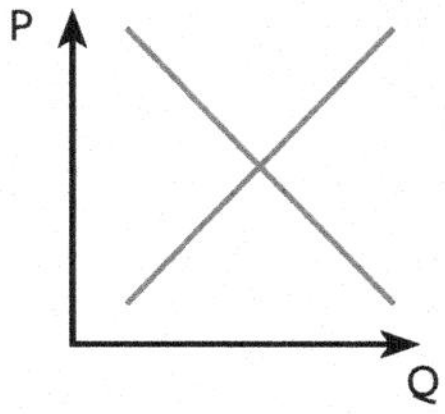 | |
| Coffee (for dunking your doughnut) rises in price | | 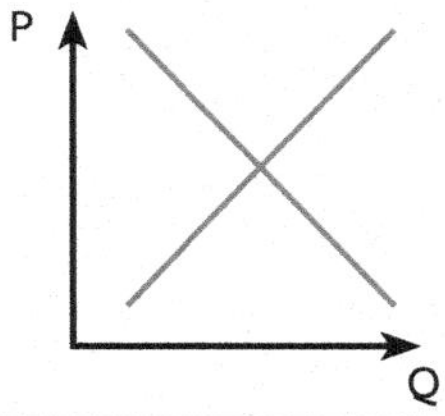 | |
| The oil that doughnuts are fried in rises in price | | 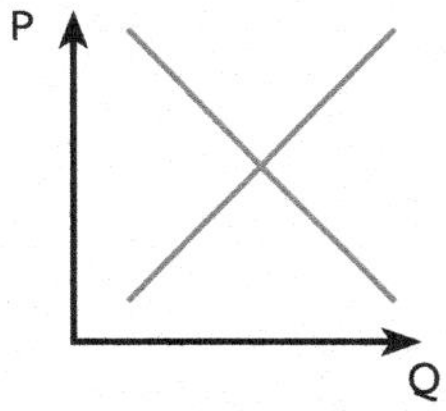 | |
| | Price of a substitute rises | 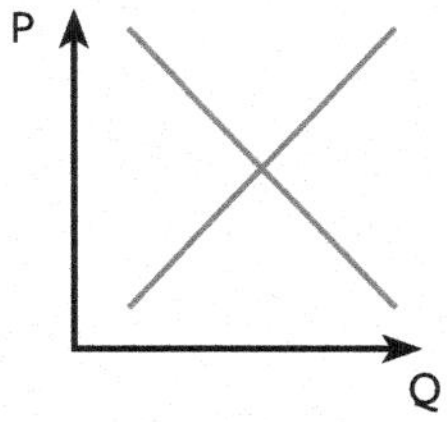 | |
| | | 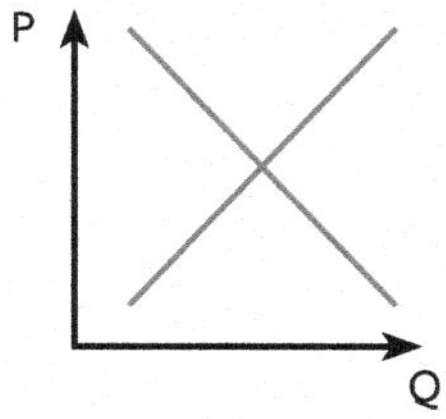 | This is an increase in *supply*. |
| Heat efficient burners for cooking oil are developed | | 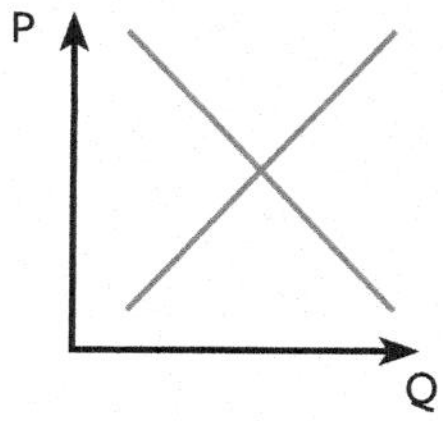 | |

Consumer, producer & government choices using supply and demand

ISBN: 9780170193955

Economics for NCEA Level One

ACTIVITY

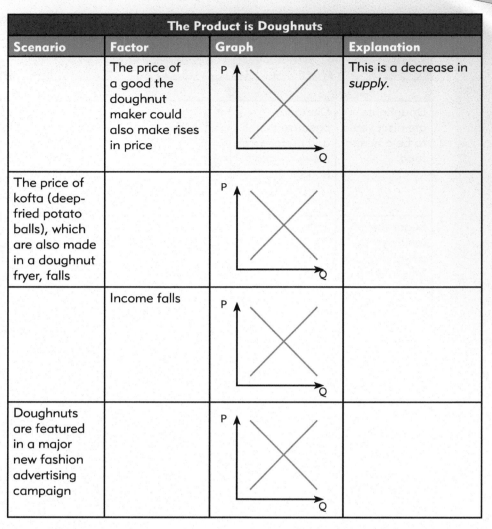

| The Product is Doughnuts | | | |
|---|---|---|---|
| **Scenario** | **Factor** | **Graph** | **Explanation** |
| | The price of a good the doughnut maker could also make rises in price | | This is a decrease in *supply*. |
| The price of kofta (deep-fried potato balls), which are also made in a doughnut fryer, falls | | | |
| | Income falls | | |
| Doughnuts are featured in a major new fashion advertising campaign | | | |

**4** Copy and complete the following table to show what would happen to the equilibrium price and quantity of woollen jerseys (in the short-term) in each of the scenarios.

| Scenario | Equilibrium price | Equilibrium quantity |
|---|---|---|
| Advertising makes woollen jerseys popular | | |
| Climatic conditions become warmer | | |
| Nylon fibre becomes cheaper | | |
| Wool prices soar | | |

**5** Real-life economics: Use supply and demand theory to explain the following events:
- The salaries of accountants continue to rise.
- House rentals are higher in Auckland than Huntly.
- Pinenuts cost $45 per kilogram (which is very expensive!).
- Salaries for shop assistants rise more slowly than salaries for computer experts.
- Gold is expensive and continues to rise.

ISBN: 9780170193955

# 20 ▪ Flow-on effects of consumer and producer choices

## By the end of this unit you will be able to:

- Explain how the market responds to changes in consumer and producer choices.
- Explain the flow-on effects to society of changes in consumer and producer choices.

In previous units we have seen that consumers and producers directly impact the market by making different choices. The Supply and Demand model can be used to illustrate the impact of these changes in choices on the market.

Equilibrium price and quantity changes when consumers make different choices because the demand changes. Equilibrium price and quantity can also change when producers make different choices because their supply changes.

Changes in demand and supply will result in a change in equilibrium. It is important to understand how the market is able to move from the original equilibrium to the new equilibrium in response to choice changes.

## Responding to changing choices

The diagram below shows the market for strawberries after stormy weather hit the strawberry fields just prior to harvest. The storm has reduced supply. We can see that the market will respond with a higher equilibrium price and smaller equilibrium quantity.

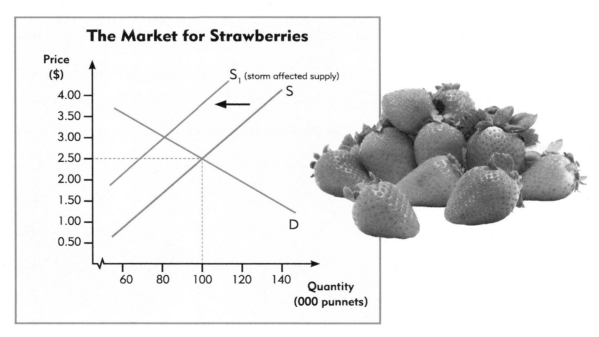

This is because at the original equilibrium price of $2.50 a punnet there will be a shortage of strawberries in the market. This will cause consumers to begin bidding up the price of strawberries, as they try to secure strawberries

ISBN: 9780170193955

for themselves. This will cause the quantity demanded to fall from 100 000 punnets and the quantity supplied to rise from 60 000 punnets until, at the new equilibrium price of $3.00 a punnet, the quantity demanded equals the quantity supplied (80 000 punnets).

This process is known as **market forces restoring market equilibrium.**

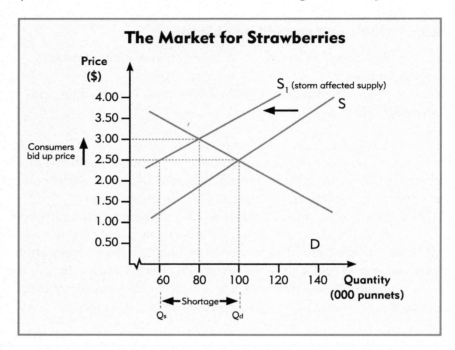

The Market for Strawberries

If the demand for strawberries decreased due to decreased income, the demand curve would shift to the left. At the original price there would be a surplus. Therefore price will drop, the quantity demanded rises and the quantity supplied falls until equilibrium is reached and the market has cleared.

## ACTIVITY

**1** Explain what is meant by the statement 'Markets are always either at or on their way to equilibrium'.

**2** Use the graph below to explain how the market will return to equilibrium.

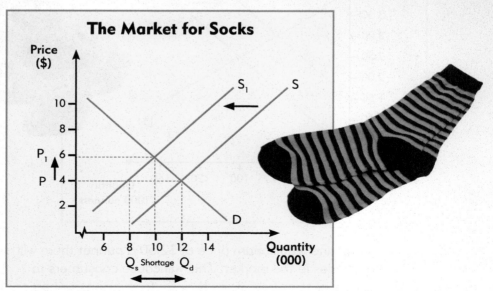

The Market for Socks

ISBN: 9780170193955

ACTIVITY

**3** Assess the following student responses to question **2** and answer the questions that follow.

**Viliami:** 'The current price is below the equilibrium price of $6. This creates a shortage of socks (4000 socks). Consumers cannot get enough socks at this price so they bid the price up. This will cause the quantity demanded to fall and the quantity supplied to rise until quantity demanded equals quantity demanded (10000 socks) at the equilibrium price of $6, and equilibrium is restored.'

**Kelly:** 'The market forces will force the market to return to equilibrium because this is where supply equals demand and the market is clear.'

**Tama:** 'The price is lower than equilibrium, there is an excess. This excess creates pressure within the market because they want to clear the market so that prices will rise until quantity supplied equals quantity demanded (at 10000 socks).'

**a** Identify the best answer.
**b** What does this answer have that the other answers do not have?
**c** Are there any other details that this student could have included?

# Flow-on effects

Previous units have shown how changes in consumer and producer choices impact on the equilibrium price and quantity. Every decision by consumers and producers has **flow-on effects** to society. Other people are affected by decisions that consumers and producers make.

The quantity of a good or service bought and sold in the market affect the quantity of resources required to make that good or service.

We have already used the following diagram to illustrate the production process:

**Inputs** $\longrightarrow$ **Production Processes** $\longrightarrow$ **Outputs**
**Resources** **Goods and services**

Increasing output requires a greater quantity of resources to produce that output. Increasing inputs deplete resources at a faster rate. More output can result in more pollution.

ISBN: 9780170193955

Economics for NCEA Level One

**CASE STUDY**

# Palm oil and chocolate

One natural resource that illustrates the flow-on effects of changes in producer decisions on the market is palm oil used in chocolate production.

'... [palm oils's] chief virtue is that it is cheap. The oil palm trees that produce the plum-sized drupes are a wonder of biology. They produce more vegetable oil per acre than any other crop, by far. Coconuts produce about half as much oil per acre, and canola and soybeans a mere tenth of that amount ... that high yield is a primary reason why palm oil usually costs a quarter to a third less than soybean oil.' (Source: www.startribune.com)

Cocoa butter has been replaced by palm oil in making chocolate. This is because palm oil is cheaper. The effect of this is shown on the graph below.

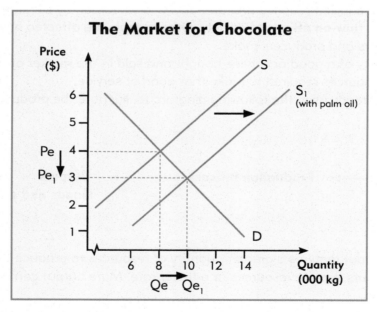

**The Market for Chocolate**

Lower costs of production due to the use of palm oil have resulted in an increase in the supply of chocolate. It is shown as a shift of the supply curve to the right.

ISBN: 9780170193955

Consumer, producer & government choices using supply and demand

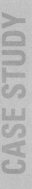

This has the effect of changing the equilibrium. The equilibrium price has fallen from $4 to $3 per kilogram. The equilibrium quantity has risen from 8000 to 10 000 kg per week

Chocolate manufacturers are able to sell more chocolate at a lower price because they have lowered their costs of production and increased their supply.

Doing this will also increase the amount of palm oil needed, therefore production of palm oil will need to increase.

'Palm oil is estimated to be in one in every 10 products we buy at the supermarket and in an astounding one in every four if we choose best-selling brands ... The rainforests of South East Asia, where oil palm plantation expansion is mostly happening, are often referred to as biodiversity hotspots; this means there is a concentration of species living closely together. Literally, hundreds of different animal species rely on these forests and several thousand species of invertebrates and plants. If we lose these forests, we will lose forever species such as the orangutan, the Sumatran tiger and the Asian elephant.' (Source: www.aucklandzoo.co.nz)

'The development of new oil palm plantations is commonly associated with social conflict and human-rights abuses. Most of the area developed is the customary land of indigenous peoples and local communities ... Indonesian laws and land acquisition procedures provide these people with very little protection. In the name of the 'national interest', communities are being forced to give up their lands against their will and without getting adequate compensation ... Many palm oil companies claim they bring work to the area, but do not always employ the local people. As a result conflicts between plantation companies and local communities are widespread and growing ... On many plantations there is heavy use of pesticides and no safety protection supplied and many of the river systems are polluted, leaving local communities with no fresh water for drinking or bathing. The pollution is also killing fish, an important food source.' (Source: www.palmoilaction.org.au)

Several environmental and indigenous rights groups have been trying to highlight the impact of increased palm oil production, and consumers have felt sympathetic to these calls. This has caused many consumers to tell chocolate manufacturers they were unhappy with this producer decision. This is shown as a decrease in demand for chocolate.

ISBN: 9780170193955

Economics for NCEA Level One

## The Market for Chocolate

Price ($)

S

Pe
Pe₁

D₁

D

Qe₁    Qe

Quantity (000 kg)

'[the manufacturer] said today that it will exclude palm oil from its chocolate, following consumer outcry over the environmental impact of palm oil plantations ... The confectionary maker said the decision to revert to its cocoa butter-only formula was a direct result of consumer feedback. (Source: www.businessgreen.com)

The manufacturer reversed its decision to use the cheaper palm oil in the face of a consumer outcry. This will cause their costs of production to rise, and supply will decrease. This is shown as a shift of the supply curve to the left, as well as a decrease in the demand for palm oil.

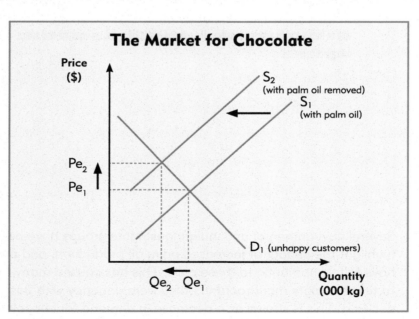

## The Market for Chocolate

Price ($)

S₂ (with palm oil removed)
S₁ (with palm oil)

Pe₂
Pe₁

D₁ (unhappy customers)

Qe₂    Qe₁

Quantity (000 kg)

ISBN: 9780170193955

Consumer, producer & government choices using supply and demand

# The recession hits the fish industry

Demand for fish has fallen due to the global recession. The effect of this is shown on the graph below. The price received by producers is lower and they sell a smaller quantity of fish.

*'[Decrease demand due to] the recession is driving structural changes to businesses, including the loss of 180 jobs at [the seafood] plant.' (Source: www.nzherald.co.nz)*

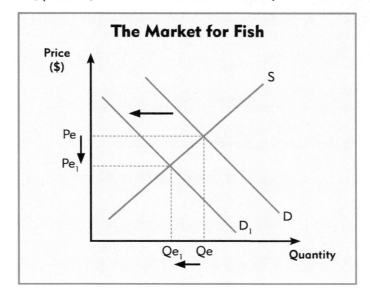

The flow-on effect of this is felt by the workers who have lost their jobs or had their pay cut. They will no longer be able to afford the same quantity of goods and services as before and will face financial constraints. They may have to find work in another region, which could impact on family members and community relationships. As incomes fall other workers may also face job losses. Local businesses will be affected by a loss of sales as these workers cut back on spending.

**1** *'Consumers are choosing Fair Trade coffee over non-Fair trade coffee. Fair trade sales grew by at 72% in New Zealand.'* (Source: www.fta.org.au). Copy the graph below and use it to answer the questions that follow.

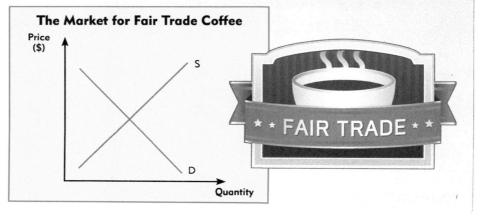

ISBN: 9780170193955

Economics for NCEA Level One

**a** Explain what is meant by the term 'Fair Trade'.

**b** Show the effect of increased consumer preference for Fair Trade coffee on your graph. Label all changes.

**c** Explain how the market will restore equilibrium following the change you have shown.

**d** List all the individuals or groups affected by changes in the Fair Trade coffee market. (Hint: Brainstorm!)

**e** Explain how Fair Trade coffee bean farmers are affected by the increased consumer preference for Fair Trade coffee.

**f** Explain how New Zealand coffee shops selling non-Free Trade coffee are affected by the increased consumer preference for Fair Trade coffee.

**2** Transport Minister: *'It will be illegal for drivers to talk or send text messages on handheld mobile phones while driving from November 1 [2009]'.* (Source: www.nzherald.co.nz). Copy the graph below and use it to answer the questions that follow.

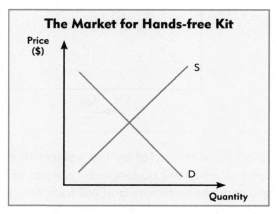

**The Market for Hands-free Kit**

**a** Show the effect of the mobile phone restriction on the market for hands-free kits for motor vehicles on your graph. Label all changes.

**b** Explain how the market will restore equilibrium following the change you have shown.

**c** List all the individuals or groups affected by changes in the mobile phone market as you can. (Hint: Brainstorm!)

**d** Explain how mobile service providers will be affected by the ban on hand-held mobile phone use in cars.

**e** Explain how employees of hands-free kit manufacturers may be affected by the ban on using hand-held mobile phones while driving.

ISBN: 9780170193955

# 21 ▪ Government choices: Price controls and the market equilibrium

**By the end of this unit you will be able to:**

• Define minimum price and maximum prices.
• Use the Supply and Demand Model to illustrate the government use of price controls on the market.
• Explain how the market responds to changes in government choices regarding price controls.
• Explain the flow-on effects to society of changes in government choices regarding price controls.

The New Zealand government is involved in the economy in a range of different ways: as a regulator in that they make laws; as a tax collector; as an owner of enterprises, for example they are the majority stakeholder of Air New Zealand; and as a provider of jobs, employment benefits, medical care, education and armed services.

Government has to make choices when trying to achieve their different economic and social policy goals. A goal may be, for example, to improve the health outcomes for New Zealanders. They could try to achieve this goal through a variety of different ways.

• Put an extra tax on cigarettes and alcohol, which is designed to discourage New Zealanders from buying these goods.
• Make it illegal to sell cigarettes to anyone under the age of 18, which is designed to stop young New Zealanders from buying these goods.
• Provide free visits to GP's for children under the age of six, which is designed to ensure young children see a doctor as often as necessary and before any health issues worsen.
• Subsidise certain medicines, which is designed to ensure more people can afford the medicine they need.
• Advertise the positive effects of exercise and healthy diet, which is designed to encourage healthy choices in New Zealand households.

Some of the tools that a government can use to influence consumer or producer behaviour, impact directly on the price of a good or service, and therefore influence the quantities of the good or service that can be bought or sold. These tools include:

ISBN: 9780170193955

Economics for NCEA Level One

1   Price controls, where the government sets a limit on the price of a good or service. There are **price maximums** and **price minimums**.
2   Subsidies.
3   Indirect taxes.

In this unit we will address the significance of government choices regarding price controls.

## Price maximums

This is when the government imposes an upper limit or the highest price that a good or service may be sold for. It is illegal to sell the product at a price higher than the price maximum. As this is the highest price possible it is sometimes called a price 'ceiling'.

By setting an uppermost limit on price the government is trying to keep the good or service affordable. The government may consider it a merit good. A merit good is a good or service that is considered beneficial by society. As the particular good or service is beneficial the government wants to make sure as many households as possible can afford them.

The aim of a price maximum is to lower prices to make the good or service more affordable for consumers. Price controls are implemented to stop the market reaching equilibrium. Therefore, a price maximum set above equilibrium will have no effect – the price will fall until equilibrium is reached.  The impact of a price maximum can be illustrated using the Supply and Demand Model.

CASE STUDY

### The price of bread

The government sets a price maximum on bread of $2 a loaf. The previous market equilibrium was $3. Unfortunately, by lowering the price the quantity supplied falls from 15 000 to 10 000 loaves while the quantity demanded has risen from 15 000 to 20 000 loaves, creating a shortage of 10 000 loaves.

Bread is now more affordable but there are not enough loaves on sale. In fact, there are even fewer loaves on sale after the price maximum than

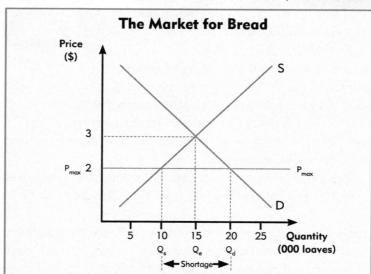

**The Market for Bread**

ISBN: 9780170193955

Consumer, producer & government choices using supply and demand

CASE STUDY

before, therefore less people can obtain the bread after the government intervention. The shortage continues – it is illegal for the price to rise to the market equilibrium – and the market does not clear.

One possible flow-on effect of this is consumers trying to pay a higher price on a **black market** to ensure they obtain bread. A black market is an illegal market, and can include markets where illegal products are bought and sold.

Black markets caused by price maximums are slightly different since the product itself may not be not illegal, however, it is an illegal market because the good is being sold at an illegal price.

*A price maximum is an unsuccessful intervention in the market.*

## ACTIVITY

Use the following market demand and supply schedules to plot the market for cycle helmets diagram and use it to answer the questions that follow.

| Market Demand Schedule for Cycle Helmets | |
|---|---|
| Price ($) | Quantity (monthly) |
| 100 | 1 000 |
| 90 | 1 200 |
| 80 | 1 400 |
| 70 | 1 600 |
| 60 | 1 800 |
| 50 | 2 000 |
| 40 | 2 200 |
| 30 | 2 400 |

| Market Supply Schedule for Cycle Helmets | |
|---|---|
| Price ($) | Quantity (monthly) |
| 100 | 2 800 |
| 90 | 2 400 |
| 80 | 2 000 |
| 70 | 1 600 |
| 60 | 1 200 |
| 50 | 800 |
| 40 | 400 |
| 30 | 100 |

**a** Clearly show and label a price maximum of $50 on your diagram.
**b** Clearly show and label the excess generated by the price maximum.
**c** Calculate the size of the excess.
**d** Explain why the market does not clear.
**e** Calculate the total sales at market equilibrium.
**f** Calculate the total sales after the price maximum was imposed.
**g** Explain why the government would impose a price maximum.
**h** Use you answers to **e** and **f** to outline how successful this strategy has been in achieving the government's goal.
**i** Explain what would happen if the government changed the price maximum to $100.

ISBN: 9780170193955

# Price minimums

This is where the limit imposed by the government is the lowest price the good may be sold for. As this is the lowest possible price it is sometimes called a price floor.

By setting a lowermost limit the government is trying to ensure higher returns to producers. This type intervention was used in the past to help New Zealand farmers.

Its impact can be illustrated using the Supply and Demand model.

## Too much butter

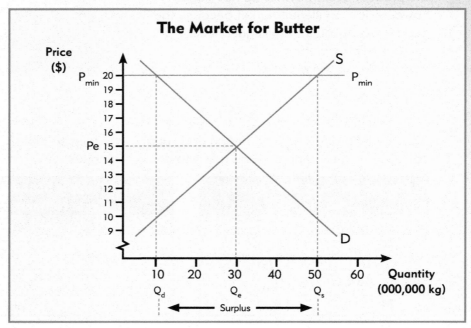

**The Market for Butter**

The government sets a price minimum on butter of $20 per kilogram. In our example the previous market equilibrium was $15. Unfortunately, by raising the minimum price the quantity supplied also rises from 30 000 000 kg to 50 000 000 kg, while the quantity demanded falls from 30 000 000 kg to 10 000 000 kg, creating a surplus of 40 000 000 kg.

The price of butter is higher but consumers are not buying it. Fewer people can afford the good after government intervention than before. The surplus continues because it is illegal for the price to fall back to the market equilibrium, and the market does not clear.

One possible flow-on effect of this price minimum is that producers begin to amass huge stockpiles. In the 1970 and 80s, when minimum prices were guaranteed to farmers, huge stockpiles accumulated and were so large they were referred to as a butter mountain or a wine lake. It can result in producers dumping unsold product.

*A price minimum is an unsuccessful intervention in the market.*

Remember, price controls are used to prevent the market from returning to equilibrium, so a price minimum set below equilibrium will have no effect – the price will simply rise until it reaches equilibrium.

ISBN: 9780170193955

As both price maximums and minimums are unsuccessful interventions they are seldom used anymore.

Consumer, producer & government choices using supply and demand

ACTIVITY

Use the following market demand and supply schedules to plot the market for pre-mixed alcoholic drinks and use it to answer the questions that follow.

| Market Demand Schedule for Pre-mixed Alcoholic Drinks, per Week | |
| --- | --- |
| Price ($) | Quantity (can) |
| 10.00 | 325 |
| 9.50 | 350 |
| 9.00 | 375 |
| 8.50 | 400 |
| 8.00 | 425 |
| 7.50 | 450 |
| 7.00 | 475 |

| Market Supply Schedule for Pre-mixed Alcoholic Drinks, per Week | |
| --- | --- |
| Price($) | Quantity (can) |
| 10.00 | 475 |
| 9.50 | 450 |
| 9.00 | 425 |
| 8.50 | 400 |
| 8.00 | 375 |
| 7.50 | 350 |
| 7.00 | 325 |

a Clearly show and label a price minimum of $9.50 on your diagram.
b Clearly show and label the excess generated by the price minimum.
c Calculate the size of the excess.
d Explain why the market does not clear.
e Calculate the total sales at market equilibrium.
f Calculate the total sales after the price minimum was imposed.
g Explain why the government would impose a price minimum.
h Use your answers from e and f to outline how successful their strategy has been.
i Explain what would happen if the government changed the price minimum to $7.50.

ISBN: 9780170193955

Economics for NCEA Level One

ISBN: 9780170193955

# 22 ▪ Government choices: Subsidies and taxes, and the market equilibrium

**By the end of this unit you will be able to:**

• Define subsides.
• Distinguish between direct and indirect taxes.
• Explain how government choices involving subsidies and taxes affect the market.
• Illustrate these choices using the Supply and Demand model.
• Explain how the market responds to changes in government choices.

More sophisticated forms of government intervention include subsidies and indirect taxes.

## Subsidies

A **subsidy** is a **transfer payment** from the government to producers that has the effect of lowering their costs of production. A transfer payment is like a gift from the government, which does not expect anything in return.

Since subsidies effectively lower the costs of production, supply is increased. The graph below shows the market for skateboard helmets.

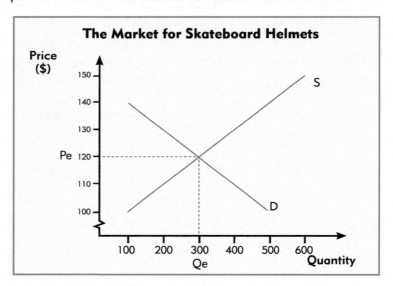

**The Market for Skateboard Helmets**

The equilibrium price is $120 and equilibrium quantity is 300 skateboard helmets.

| Supply Schedule for Skateboard Helmets | |
|---|---|
| Price ($) | Quantity |
| 100 | 100 |
| 110 | 200 |
| 120 | 300 |
| 130 | 400 |
| 140 | 500 |
| 150 | 600 |

The supply schedule tells us that:
- When the skateboard helmet supplier receives $100 they are willing to supply 100 skateboard helmets
- When the skateboard helmet supplier receives $110 they are willing to supply 200 skateboard helmets
- When the skateboard helmet supplier receives $120 they are willing to supply 300 skateboard helmets
- When the skateboard helmet supplier receives $130 they are willing to supply 400 skateboard helmets
- When the skateboard helmet supplier receives $140 they are willing to supply 500 skateboard helmets
- When the skateboard helmet supplier receives $150 they are willing to supply 600 skateboard helmets.

The government then introduces a $10 subsidy to producers of skateboard helmets for every skateboard helmet supplied. So now:
- Consumers pay $100 and the government adds $10 so the producer receives $110, from the schedule we can see the producers will supply 200 skateboard helmets
- Consumers pay $110 and the government adds $10 so the producer receives $120, from the schedule we can see the producers will supply 300 skateboard helmets
- Consumers pay $120 and the government adds $10 so the producer receives $130, from the schedule we can see the producers will supply 400 skateboard helmets
- Consumers pay $130 and the government adds $10 so the producer receives $140, from the schedule we can see the producers will supply 500 skateboard helmets
- Consumers pay $140 and the government adds $10 so the producer receives $150, from the schedule we can see the producers will supply 600 skateboard helmets.

We can construct a new supply schedule using this information and draw the new supply for skateboard helmets after the subsidy has been introduced. The subsidy has the effect of increasing helmet supply.

| New Supply Schedule for Skateboard Helmets ||
|---|---|
| Price ($) | Quantity |
| 100 | 200 |
| 110 | 300 |
| 120 | 400 |
| 130 | 500 |
| 140 | 600 |

ISBN: 9780170193955

Economics for NCEA Level One

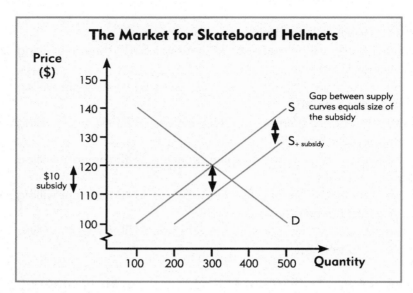

Note that the *vertical distance* or gap – between the old supply curve and the supply curve after the subsidy has been introduced – is exactly the same size as the subsidy.

This means that you can draw the supply curve with the subsidy without doing all of the working we did on page 145. Use the size of the subsidy to measure the vertical distance between the two curves and draw a new curve.

To do this accurately you need to mark two points below the old supply curve and then join them using a ruler.

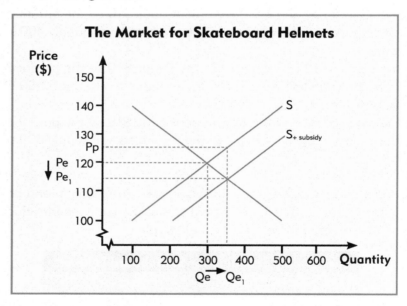

Once you have carefully drawn your new supply curve with the subsidy, you need to accurately label and interpret the graph.

The new equilibrium price (Qe) is the price paid by consumers for the skateboard helmets. Producers receive this price *plus* the subsidy (the vertical distance or the gap). We find this amount by continuing the dotted line up from the new equilibrium quantity (Qe₁) to the old supply curve and join them to the price axis using a horizontal dotted line.

This is *not* the market price, but the amount that is received by producers for each unit sold. We have labelled it Pp, with the subscript p indicating producers.

Note that the $10 subsidy has been paid to the producer. Part of this has been passed onto the consumer through the decrease in equilibrium price – the price does not fall by the full $10. The producer receives the new equilibrium price plus the subsidy.

ISBN: 9780170193955

Consumer, producer & government choices using supply and demand

1 Use the following supply and demand schedules to construct the market for asthma inhalers.

| Demand Schedule for Asthma Inhalers, per Week | |
|---|---|
| Price ($) | Quantity demanded |
| 5 | 9000 |
| 6 | 8000 |
| 7 | 7000 |
| 8 | 6000 |
| 9 | 5000 |
| 10 | 4000 |
| 11 | 3000 |
| 12 | 2000 |
| 13 | 1000 |

| Supply Schedule for Asthma Inhalers, per Week | |
|---|---|
| Price ($) | Quantity demanded |
| 5 | 1000 |
| 6 | 2000 |
| 7 | 3000 |
| 8 | 4000 |
| 9 | 5000 |
| 10 | 6000 |
| 11 | 7000 |
| 12 | 8000 |
| 13 | 9000 |

2 Show the effect of a subsidy ($3) on your diagram.

3 Fully label your graph using standard notation to illustrate the effect of the subsidy.

4 Identify the price paid by consumers and the price received by producers.

## A worked example of skateboard helmet subsidy

### Key formula
TOTAL REVENUE is equal to PRICE multiplied by QUANTITY (TR = P x Q).

Calculating the total revenue earned by producers *before* the subsidy is given. Note: Use the original equilibrium.

$$
\begin{aligned}
\text{total revenue} &= \text{price received} && \times && \text{number of units sold} \\
&= P && \times && Q \\
&= Pe && \times && Qe \\
&= 120 && \times && 300 \\
&= \$36\,000
\end{aligned}
$$

Calculating the total revenue earned by producers *after* the subsidy

$$
\begin{aligned}
\text{total revenue} &= \text{price received} && \times && \text{number of units sold} \\
&= (Pe_1 + \text{subsidy}) && \times && Qe_1 \\
&= (\$115 + \$10) && \times && 350 \\
&= \$125 && \times && 350 \\
&= \$43\,750
\end{aligned}
$$

ISBN: 9780170193955

Economics for NCEA Level One

**CASE STUDY**

Calculating the total cost of the subsidy to the government

total government  =  subsidy per unit    x    number of units sold
spending           =  subsidy           x    $Qe_1$
                =  $10             x    350
                =  $3 500

Calculating the total spending of consumers after the subsidy

total spending   =  price paid        x    quantity bought
               =  $Pe_1$          x    $Qe_1$
               =  $115         x    350
               =  $40 250

**Check your work**

total expenditure  +  total subsidy paid  =  total revenue earned by
by consumers          by government        producers

    $40 250      +      $3 500        =     $43 750

After a subsidy has been introduced and the supply increases, consumers are able to buy a greater quantity of the good or service at a lower price. The subsidy does not create a shortage when it lowers the price because the subsidy creates a new equilibrium. The market will clear.

*This is a successful government intervention.*

A subsidy graph can also be used to find out how much the subsidy will cost the government in total, how much the producer receives for the good in total, and how much the consumer has to pay in total.

The government is paying for the goods to be cheaper. This is expensive for them, so they will only do this for merit goods. Merit goods are goods and services that the government believes are of beneficial to you.

**ACTIVITY**

1 List as many goods or services as you can that you think are merit goods.

2 Choose two goods or services from your list and outline how the government tries to encourage consumers to use them.

3 Using the asthma inhalers subsidy scenario on page 147, calculate:
   a   Total revenue earned by producers *before* the subsidy is given.
   b   Total revenue earned by the producers *after* the subsidy is given.
   c   Total cost of the subsidy to the government.
   d   Total spending of consumers *after* the subsidy.

ISBN: 9780170193955

# Sales taxes

In Unit 3 we saw that the government collects income tax from workers. In New Zealand the system is called PAYE (Pay As You Earn). Income tax is a **direct tax** because it is a tax on income or earnings. Income tax affects household income and so affects their demand.

Another major tax the government collects is sales tax. It is an **indirect tax**, which means it is a tax on consumption or spending. GST (Goods and Services Tax) is the most common form in New Zealand. Sales taxes affect supply.

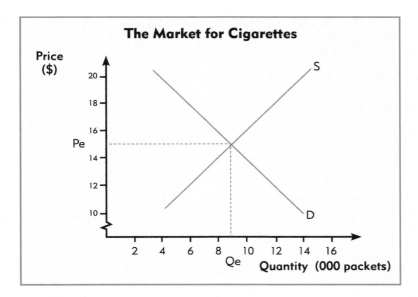

| Supply Schedule for Cigarettes | |
|---|---|
| Price ($) | Quantity (packets) |
| 10 | 4000 |
| 12 | 6000 |
| 14 | 8000 |
| 16 | 10000 |
| 18 | 12000 |
| 20 | 14000 |

The equilibrium price for cigarettes is $15 and equilibrium quantity is 9000 packets. The supply schedule tells us that:

- When the cigarette supplier receives $10 they are willing to supply 4000 cigarettes
- When the cigarette supplier receives $12 they are willing to supply 6000 cigarettes
- When the cigarette supplier receives $14 they are willing to supply 8000 cigarettes
- When the cigarette supplier receives $16 they are willing to supply 10000 cigarettes
- When the cigarette supplier receives $18 they are willing to supply 12000 cigarettes
- When the cigarette supplier receives $20 they are willing to supply 14000 cigarettes.

The government then introduces a $2 indirect tax on cigarettes. This is a $2 tax to the supplier for every cigarette packet supplied. So now:
- When consumers pay $12 the government takes $2 so the producer receives $10, from the schedule we can see the producers supply 4000 cigarettes
- When consumers pay $14 the government takes $2 so the producer receives $12, from the schedule we can see the producers supply 6000 cigarettes
- When consumers pay $16 the government takes $2 so the producer receives $14, from the schedule we can see the producers supply 8000 cigarettes
- When consumers pay $18 and the government takes $2 so the producer receives $16, from the schedule we can see the producers supply 10000 cigarettes

ISBN: 9780170193955

Economics for NCEA Level One

ISBN: 9780170193955

- When consumers pay $20 and the government takes $2 so the producer receives $18, from the schedule we can see the producers supply 12 000 cigarettes
- When consumers pay $22 and the government takes $2 so the producer receives $20, from the schedule we can see that the producers supply 14 000 cigarettes.

We can construct a new supply schedule using this information, and draw the new supply curve for cigarettes after the sales tax was introduced.

| New Supply Schedule for Cigarettes | |
| --- | --- |
| Price ($) | Quantity with tax (packets) |
| 12 | 4 000 |
| 14 | 6 000 |
| 16 | 8 000 |
| 18 | 10 000 |
| 20 | 12 000 |

A sales tax has the effect of decreasing supply. We expect this because it raises the costs of production. It creates a new equilibrium price ($Pe_1$) and quantity ($Qe_1$).

Note that the *vertical distance* or gap between the old supply curve and the supply curve after the sales tax has been introduced is exactly the same size as the sales tax. Part of the sales tax is passed onto the consumer through the increase in equilibrium price. Part of the tax burden falls to the consumer and part on the producer.

This means that we can draw the supply curve with the sales tax without doing all of the working we did above.

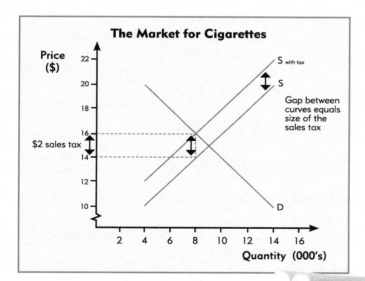

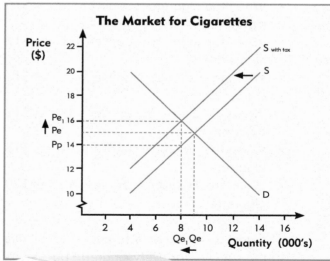

Use the size of the sales tax to measure the vertical distance between the two curves and draw a new curve. To do this accurately you need to mark two points above the old supply curve and then join them using a ruler.

Once you have accurately drawn your new supply curve to include the sales tax, you need to accurately label and interpret the graph.

The new equilibrium price is the price paid by consumers for cigarettes. Producers receive this price less the sales tax (the vertical distance or gap). We find this by moving the dotted line down from the new equilibrium quantity to the old supply curve and then drawing a dotted line horizontal to the price axis.

This is *not* the market price, but the price received by producers. We have labelled it Pp, with the lowercase p indicating producers.

Consumer, producer & government choices using supply and demand

## ACTIVITY

1 Use the following supply and demand schedules to construct a market diagram.

| Demand Schedule for High Fat Confectionery, per week | |
|---|---|
| Price ($) | Quantity demanded |
| 1 | 9 000 |
| 2 | 8 000 |
| 3 | 7 000 |
| 4 | 6 000 |
| 5 | 5 000 |
| 6 | 4 000 |
| 7 | 3 000 |
| 8 | 2 000 |
| 9 | 1 000 |

| Supply Schedule for High Fat Confectionery, per week | |
|---|---|
| Price ($) | Quantity supplied |
| 1 | 1 000 |
| 2 | 2 000 |
| 3 | 3 000 |
| 4 | 4 000 |
| 5 | 5 000 |
| 6 | 6 000 |
| 7 | 7 000 |
| 8 | 8 000 |
| 9 | 9 000 |

2 Show the effect of a sales tax ($2) on your diagram.

3 Fully label your graph using standard notation to identify the price paid by consumers and the price received by producers.

4 Identify the size of the sales tax on your diagram using a double headed arrow and label.

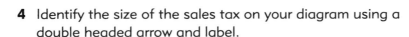

ISBN: 9780170193955

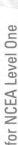

Economics for NCEA Level One

**CASE STUDY**

## A worked example of cigarette sales tax

Refer to the example on page 149–150.

**Key formula**

TOTAL REVENUE is equal to PRICE multiplied by QUANTITY ($TR = P \times Q$).

Calculating the total revenue earned by producers *before* the sales tax is given. Note: Use the original equilibrium.

| total revenue | = | price received | x | number of units sold |
|---|---|---|---|---|
| | = | P | x | Q |
| | = | Pe | x | Qe |
| | = | 15 | x | 9000 |
| | = | $135000 | | |

Calculating the total revenue earned by producers *after* the sales tax

| total revenue | = | price received | x | number of units sold |
|---|---|---|---|---|
| | = | $(Pe_1 - \text{sales tax})$ | x | $Qe_1$ |
| | = | ($16 – $2) | x | 8000 |
| | = | $14 | x | 8000 |
| | = | $112000 | | |

Calculating the total income earned from the sales tax by the government

| total spending | = | sales tax per unit | x | number of units sold |
|---|---|---|---|---|
| | = | sales tax | x | $Qe_1$ |
| | = | $2 | x | 8000 |
| | = | $16000 | | |

Calculating the total spending of consumers *after* the sales tax

| total spending | = | price paid | x | quantity bought |
|---|---|---|---|---|
| | = | $Pe_1$ | x | $Qe_1$ |
| | = | $16 | x | 8000 |
| | = | $128000 | | |

**Check your work**

| total expenditure by consumers | – | total tax collected by government | = | total revenue earned by producers |
|---|---|---|---|---|
| $128000 | – | $16000 | = | $112000 |

After a sales tax has been introduced and the supply has decreased, consumers buy a smaller quantity of goods at a higher price. The sales tax does not create a surplus when it raises the price because it creates a new equilibrium. The market will clear.

*This is a successful government intervention.*

Although sales taxes make the good or service more expensive for the consumer, the government uses the tax to collect revenue. The government can then use the revenue to fund other activities such as medical research associated with smoking and cancer, anti-smoking advertisements or quit smoking services, or any other government activity.

ISBN: 9780170193955

A sales tax has the effect of lowering consumption by making goods more expensive. Government may put extra sales taxes (an excise tax) on goods they consider to be demerit goods. These are goods and services that the government believes are bad for us.

The sales tax graph can also be used to find out how much a sales tax will cost the government in total, how much the producer receives for the good in total, and how much the consumer has to pay in total.

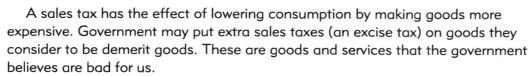
## ACTIVITY

1 For the *High Fat Confectionary* scenario described in the previous activity on page 151, calculate:
   a Total revenue earned by producers *before* the sales tax.
   b Total revenue earned by the producers *after* the sales tax.
   c Total revenue of the sales tax paid to the government.
   d Total spending of consumers *after* the sales tax.

2 Define a merit good.

3 Define a demerit good.

4 List as many goods or services as you can that you think are demerit goods.

5 Chose two goods or services from your list and outline how the government tries to discourage consumers from using them.

6 Classify the following as either a merit or demerit good:
   a seatbelts
   b lead petrol
   c cigarettes
   d cycle helmets
   e literacy
   f doctor's visits
   g vaccinations
   h education
   i alcohol
   j fruit and vegetables
   k illicit drugs

7 Plot the market for calcium-enriched milk on a graph and use it to answer the questions that follow.

| Market Demand Schedule for Calcium-enriched Milk, per week | | Market Supply Schedule for Calcium-enriched Milk, per week | |
| --- | --- | --- | --- |
| Price ($) | Quantity (000 litres) | Price ($) | Quantity (000 litres) |
| 2.00 | 100 | 2.00 | 160 |
| 1.90 | 110 | 1.90 | 150 |
| 1.80 | 120 | 1.80 | 140 |
| 1.70 | 130 | 1.70 | 130 |
| 1.60 | 140 | 1.60 | 120 |
| 1.50 | 150 | 1.50 | 110 |
| 1.40 | 160 | 1.40 | 100 |

   a Show the effect of the government imposing a $0.30 subsidy.
   b Describe what has happened to equilibrium price and quantity.

ISBN: 9780170193955

**c** Calculate the following:

  **i)** Total producer revenue *before* the subsidy was imposed.

  **ii)** Total producer revenue *after* the subsidy was imposed.

  **iii)** Total cost of the subsidy to the government.

  **iv)** Total consumer expenditure *before* the subsidy was imposed.

  **v)** Total consumer expenditure *after* the subsidy was imposed.

  **vi)** The percentage change in total producer revenue.

  **vii)** The percentage change in consumer expenditure.

**d** Explain why the government would pay a subsidy.

**e** Explain the relationship between total revenue after the subsidy, government spending on the subsidy, and consumer expenditure.

**8** Plot the market for tobacco on a graph and use it to answer the questions that follow.

| Market Demand Schedule for Tobacco, per week | | Market Supply Schedule for Tobacco, per week | |
| --- | --- | --- | --- |
| Price ($) | Quantity (000 packets) | Price ($) | Quantity (000 packets) |
| 12 | 100 | 12 | 160 |
| 11 | 110 | 11 | 150 |
| 10 | 120 | 10 | 140 |
| 9 | 130 | 9 | 130 |
| 8 | 140 | 8 | 120 |
| 7 | 150 | 7 | 110 |
| 6 | 160 | 6 | 100 |

**a** Show the effect of the government imposing a $3 tax.

**b** Describe what has happened to equilibrium price and quantity.

**c** Calculate the following:

  **i)** Total producer revenue *before* the tax was imposed.

  **ii)** Total producer revenue *after* the tax was imposed.

  **iii)** The total revenue collected by the government.

  **iv)** Total consumer expenditure *before* the tax was imposed.

  **v)** Total consumer expenditure *after* the tax was imposed.

  **vi)** The percentage change in total producer revenue.

  **vii)** The percentage change in consumer expenditure.

  **viii)** Total amount of tax paid by producer.

  **ix)** Total amount of tax paid by consumer.

**d** Explain why the government would impose an indirect tax.

**e** Explain the relationship between producers' total revenue after the tax, government revenue from the tax, and consumer expenditure.

**9** Explain why taxes and subsidies are more successful than price minimums and price maximums.

ACTIVITY

**10** The following graph shows the effect of a sales tax on a market. Match the letters to identify the areas on the graph:

    **a**    total revenue for producers before the tax was imposed

    **b**    total revenue for producers after the tax was imposed

    **c**    total revenue collected by the government

    **d**    total consumer expenditure before the tax was imposed

    **e**    total consumer expenditure after the tax was imposed

    **f**    amount of the tax per unit.

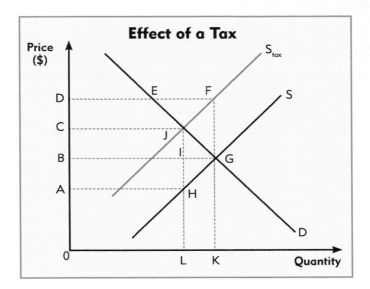

**11** The graph below shows the effect of a subsidy on a market. Match the letters to identify the areas on the graph:

    **a**    total revenue for producers before the subsidy was paid

    **b**    total revenue for producers after the subsidy was paid

    **c**    total spending by the government

    **d**    total consumer expenditure before the subsidy was paid

    **e**    total consumer expenditure after the subsidy was paid

    **f**    amount of the subsidy per unit.

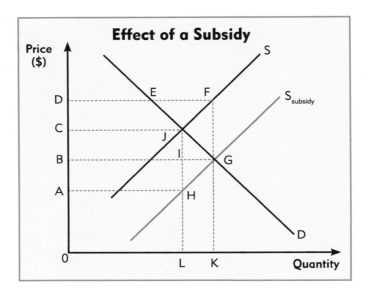

Consumer, producer & government choices using supply and demand

ISBN: 9780170193955

Economics for NCEA Level One

# 23 ▪ Flow-on effects of government choices

**By the end of this unit you will be able to:**

- Explain how the market responds to changes in government choices
- Explain the flow-on effects to society of changes in government choices.

The government interventions we have studied over the last couple of units have demonstrated the effect of manipulating the market. Certain changes (subsidies and sales taxes) have been successful because they created new market equilibriums, and others (price maximums and price minimums) have not because they have pushed producers and consumers away from the market equilibrium which creates shortages or surpluses within the market.

Government subsidies are paid for with tax dollars, while sales taxes earn the government revenue at the expense of consumers and producers. These interventions have flow-on effects on consumers, producers and even on the government itself.

## SuperGold cards

The New Zealand government chooses to subsidise the cost of public transport for superannuitants through the SuperGold card, which is a free discount and concession card available to New Zealand residents aged 65 years or over.

This lowers the cost of the public transport and so supply of public transport increases. The equilibrium price has fallen while the equilibrium quantity has risen.

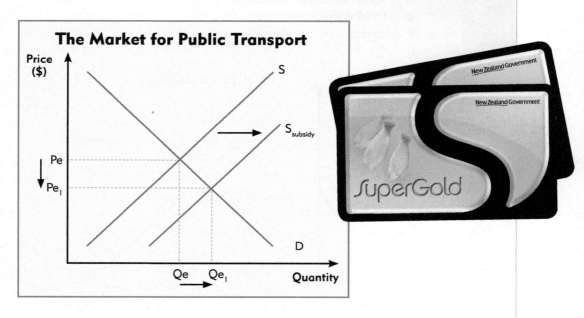

The Market for Public Transport

ISBN: 9780170193955

Consumer, producer & government choices using supply and demand

## CASE STUDY

This government choice has several flow-on effects.

**1** Consumers of public transport:
- Superannuitants. They can access a greater amount of public transport at a lower price.
- Other public transport users. They may benefit from a greater range of routes and services since increased numbers of older travellers require more public transport services.

**2** Producers of public transport:
- They are receiving a higher price (equilibrium price plus the subsidy) and are selling a larger quantity of tickets because of the subsidy, which may lead to increased employment levels in public transport, higher wages in the public transport sector or increasing numbers of bus routes.

**3** Government:
- Spending increases, but cannot be spent on other services. May have to decrease spending in other areas, such as healthcare or education.

## ACTIVITY

**1** The government is increasing the sales tax on alcohol.
- **a** Draw a fully labelled market graph illustrating the market for alcohol, including the increase in sales tax.
- **b** Use the Supply and Demand model to fully explain how an sales tax would affect (i) suppliers of alcohol, (ii) consumers of alcohol, and (iii) the government.

**2** The government is introducing a subsidy on primary school reading books.
- **a** Draw a fully labelled market graph illustrating the market for primary school reading books showing the introduced subsidy.
- **b** Use the Supply and Demand model to fully explain how a subsidy would affect (i) suppliers of primary school reading books, (ii) consumers of primary school reading books, and (iii) the government.

ISBN: 9780170193955

# 5

# Understanding different viewpoints

## 24 ▪ Balancing unlimited wants, limited resources and choice

**By the end of this unit you will be able to:**

- Explain all choices are a necessary result of having unlimited wants but only limited means or resources.
- Recognise government refers to any governing body at a national, regional or local level.
- Identify other groups who are affected by the choices made by government.
- Recognise different groups have differing viewpoints.
- Evaluate a government choice using the decision making process.

Everyone must make choices. We all have unlimited wants and only limited means or resources to satisfy these choices.

ISBN: 9780170193955

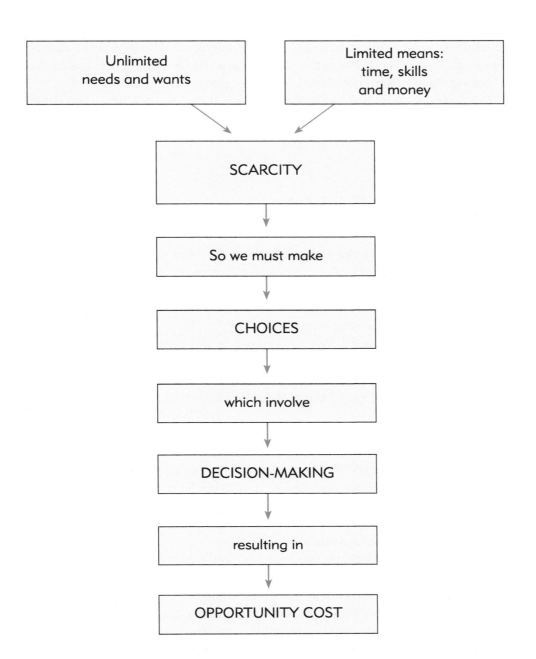

All choices affect other people or groups. Your decision to skip netball training impacts on your team and coach (and possibly on the next team you play), or your decision not to do your homework impacts on your teacher and the class in the next lesson (not to mention the impact on YOU!).

ISBN: 9780170193955

**ACTIVITY**

**1  a**  List five choices you have made today.
 **b**  List five choices your family have made this week.
 **c**  List five choices your school has made this month.
 **d**  List five choices the local council has made in the last two years.
 **e**  List five choices the central government has made in the last two years.

**2**  For each of the groups listed in the activity above, select one choice and outline the impacts of that choice on other individuals or groups.

Governments must balance the interests of everyone. The bigger the decision is, the bigger the potential impact on others could be. A small group are in charge of making decisions on behalf of a much larger group.

The best decisions are well-informed ones. If the group making the decision is to choose the best option available it needs to ensure group members fully understand the problem, as well as the impact and flow-on effects any solution may have.

## The decision making process

We can split the decision making process into six steps:

1 **Recognising there is the need to make a decision about a choice.** Why is the choice required? What are our scarce resources or our limited means? Why can we not do anything we want?
2 **Alternatives.** What are the options available? What other solutions do we have that will achieve our purpose?
3 **Identify affected groups.** Who is affected by this decision? What do *they* want to happen? What compromises are they prepared to make, that is, what is the solution that will partially satisfy the requirements of more than one group, rather than only one group benefitting. Brainstorm to generate a list of affected individual or groups.
4 **Cost and benefit analysis.** What are the costs and benefits of each of the alternative solutions and compromise solutions? What are the advantages and the disadvantages of choosing each alternative? Are some advantages or disadvantages more important than others? Step 4 allows the decision makers to explore the alternatives and gather enough information to make an informed decision. Interview affected individuals and groups to gather information to aid your decision.
5 **Rank the options.** Which is the best solution? Weigh up each alternatives costs (disadvantages) and benefits (advantages) and sort them into a ranked list: First on the list is the best solution available.
6 **Justify the decision.** This process has produced a 'best' solution. Justify why your choice is the best. Explain the costs and benefits of the decision, recognising that some costs and benefits are more significant than others.

## Recreation areas

The local city council is reviewing recreation area usage. A local playground is one of the parks under review, and there is $250 000 available to spend on changes. Two ideas that have been suggested by local residents:

- Increase the quality of the equipment and landscape the area so that more families can use the space.
- Remove the old playground equipment entirely and build a new skateboard park for local teenagers.

ISBN: 9780170193955

**CASE STUDY**

The council is using the six step decision making process outlined above to reach a decision:

1 **Why is a choice necessary?**
   The council has only a fixed number of recreation spaces available to meet the needs of the entire community. In addition to this they have a limited budget with which to provide facilities in these recreation areas. The limited budget and limited physical areas are scarce resources.

   Local government must choose how to best meet the needs of the community with only these given resources.

2 **What are the alternatives?**
   The council has investigated the local community and arrived at two options:

   • Increase the quality of the equipment and landscape the area so that more families can use the space.
   • Remove the old playground equipment entirely and build a new skateboard park for locals.

   The investigation also revealed a compromise position that could be considered further:

   • The local teenagers have indicated that they would be happy to have a smaller skate park and share the area with the playground if some particularly challenging and exciting ramps can be built.

3 **Who is affected?** Playground users, local residents near the park, skateboarders and other users of the park.

4 **What are the costs and benefits for each of the identified alternatives and the compromise above?**
   **Alternative 1:** Increase the quality of the equipment and landscape the area so that more families can use the space.

ISBN: 9780170193955

Economics for NCEA Level One

CASE STUDY

| Costs | Benefits |
|---|---|
| 1 The playground equipment will suit only those members of the community with young children | 1 The town has a lack of suitable spaces for young families, in fact apart from two swings near the shopping centre this is the only council playground |
| 2 Most of the families in the town make good use of the facilities provided by the local playgroup (a parent volunteer run early childhood centre), which allows out of hours use of the playground area to families attending the playgroup. Most families in town (76%) are members of playgroup | 2 The town council is funding a 'Happy Families' programme aimed at getting families active and enjoying the outdoors instead of watching TV and playing computer games as part of its anti-obesity health programme. Better facilities would help with this |
| 3 The cost of landscaping and new equipment to meet OSH requirements will use the entire budget | 3 After the areas is landscaped other groups without children would be able to enjoy the space |

**Alternative 2:** Remove the old playground equipment entirely and build a new skateboard park for locals.

| Costs | Benefits |
|---|---|
| 1 The skateboard park will only be used by a small number of the total teenage population in the town | 1 The town has a lack of suitable spaces for teenagers. The only facility available is a homework club at the library funded by the council |
| 2 The nearest town built a skate park several years ago and it is now hardly used | 2 The area available to other groups to use would remain the same |
| 3 Some older residents living near the park have indicated they are unhappy with skateboarders hanging out at the park and that they would prefer young families | 3 The Police Youth Officer has indicated most of the petty crime in town is committed by teenagers with nothing to do. The skateboard park may alleviate some of this offending |

**Alternative 3:** The local teenagers have indicated that they would be happy to have a smaller skate park and share the area with the playground if some particularly challenging and exciting ramps are built.

ISBN: 9780170193955

Understanding different viewpoints

| Costs | Benefits |
|---|---|
| 1 The OSH requirements mean the 'challenging' and 'exciting' ramps desired by teenagers are not possible | 1 Increases the number of groups that could use the park and facilities |
| 2 Some parents of young children have indicated they find the teenagers' language unsuitable and would not use shared facilities | 2 Many families have both younger and older children. This arrangement would allow them to spend time together |

5 **Rank the options.** First choice: Skate park. Second choice: Shared facilities. Third choice: Playground.

6 **Justify the decision.** The council should use the funds to provide a skateboard park. The council must try to meet the needs of all members of the community. The skate park meets the needs of a group of the community that has no other facilities. Because the teenagers have extremely limited facilities, this option has been given a weighting of 7 out of 10 in importance. The benefit identified by the Police Youth Officer was given a weighting of 8 out of 10 since curbing delinquency would benefit all members of the community. The compromise position is not suitable as the teenagers would want specific ramps being available (and they would not be). The playground for families only had a weighting of 5 out of 10 even though there are only a set of swings provided by the council, and a large number of families already have access to playground facilities through the play centre. It was noted that the low numbers of skateboarders at a nearby town's skateboard park could have been due to its small size or limited range of ramps, also suggesting that a smaller skate park was not acceptable. This was rated 9 out of 10 for costs. Older resident's concerns were rated a 5 as the teenagers are members of the community as well and cannot be denied facilities they need simply because other groups do not like them.

1 Use the decision making model to make a decision regarding the following government choices:

   a The PTA usually raises $30 000 a year through their fundraising efforts. They have asked the Board of Trustees to decide on a suitable project that the money could be used for. The two alternatives the Board has suggested are (1) a class set of iphones to aid learning, or (2) new sports equipment for the gymnasium.

   b The city council has $50 000 to spend on an ART project. The two alternatives are (1) a mural on the main street, or (2) funding a youth theatre group for a year.

   c The government has to decide whether or not to allow offshore drilling for oil.

ISBN: 9780170193955

ISBN: 9780170193955

# 6

# Interdependence of sectors in the New Zealand economy

## 25 ▪ Primary, secondary and tertiary sectors and interdependence

**By the end of this unit you will be able to:**

- Define interdependence.
- Distinguish between dependence, independence and interdependence.
- Define and give examples of primary, secondary and tertiary producers.
- Explain how primary, secondary and tertiary producer sectors are interdependent.

**Interdependence** means to rely on one another or **mutual reliance**. To be independent means to be self-sufficient, and to be dependent means to rely on another. Interdependence is a significant concept in Economics. All members of an economy are interrelated, and their relationships are interdependent. This means that all participants rely on each other. To see this in action we can look at how consumption and production processes are built on interdependence.

Producers supply goods and services and can be classified according to what they produce:

- **Primary** producers are involved in the extraction or harvesting of natural resources. Examples of Primary Sector industries inlcude fishing, mining, horticulture or farming.

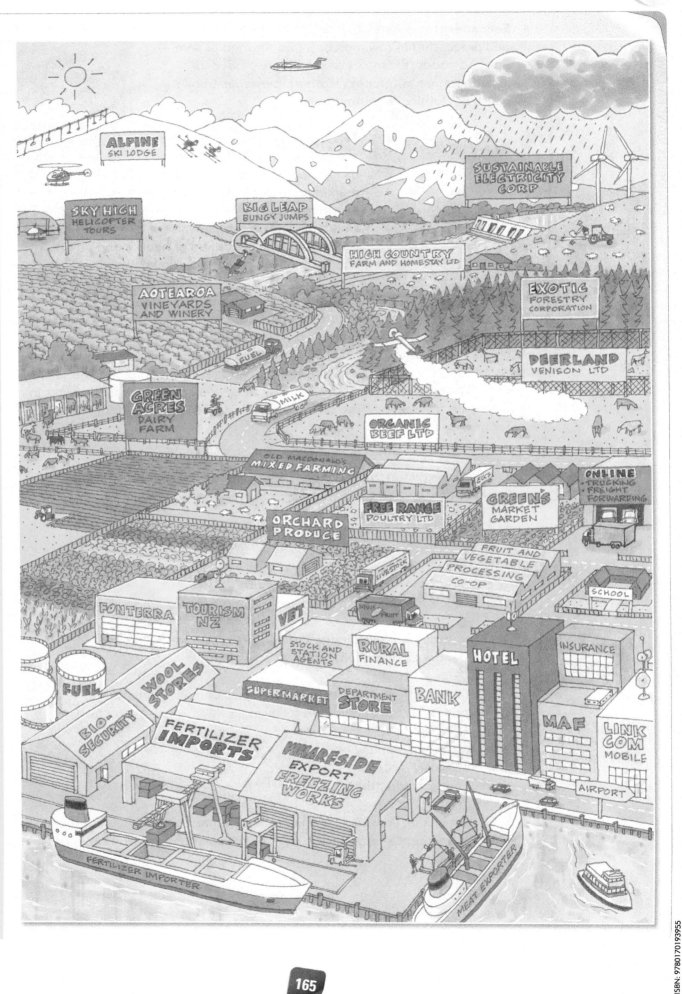

ISBN: 9780170193955

**6**

- **Secondary** producers are involved in the manufacturing and processing of raw materials into finished or semi-finished goods. Examples of secondary producers include tanneries (process leather), breweries (make beer), or clothing manufacturers.

  - **Tertiary** producers are service providers, such as finance, accounting, marketing, communication or transportation. While these services were identified in Unit 5, it is not a complete list of all services. Other services include education or health, and power, phone and water services (also known as *utilities*).

Many of the producers indicated in the illustration on page 165 rely on each other. The primary sector is relying on the secondary sector to process the raw materials they have extracted. The secondary sector is relying the primary sector to extract the raw materials so that they can process them into goods and services. The tertiary sector relies upon all three sectors to use their services in order to earn revenue and the other sectors rely on the services that the tertiary sector provides.

1   Using the picture resource on the previous page, identify all primary, all secondary and all tertiary sector producers.

2   Fully explain how the following pairs of firms are interdependent.
    a   *Pennycook Accountants* and *Vila Fisheries.*
    b   *Dylan's Fruit Shop* and *Issie's Fresh Fruit Orchard.*
    c   *Joe's Tannery* and *Gus' Beef Farm.*
    d   *Eddie's Fish and Chip Shop* and *Tukaha's Potato Processing Factory.*

3   Using examples, explain the difference between dependence, independence and interdependence.

4   Give three different and specific examples of a service the tertiary sector provides to each of the following:
    a   A horticulturist.
    b   A mining company.
    c   A farmer.
    d   A car manufacturer.

5   Draw a simple flow chart of the production process, highlighting the interdependence between the sectors, for each of the following goods and services:
    a   Bread.
    b   Education.
    c   A hamburger.

ISBN: 9780170193955

# 26 ▪ Basic circular flow

**By the end of this unit you will be able to:**

- Describe the interdependence between households and producers.
- Differentiate between real and money flows.
- Construct a two sector circular flow model.
- Explain that all resources are owned by households and earn a specific return.

Production and consumption are the most basic functions in any economy. Although the same people are doing both things, in Economics we split them according to their function, in other words, what they are doing.

The group of *all* consumers of *all* goods and services is called **household sector**, and the group of *all* producers of *all* goods is called **producer sector**. There is an interdependent relationship between the two groups, or one of mutual reliance: Households rely on firms to produce the goods and services for them to consume, and firms rely on households to provide the resources (most visibly workers or labour) required to produce those goods and services.

Interdependence can be illustrated by using the circular flow model:

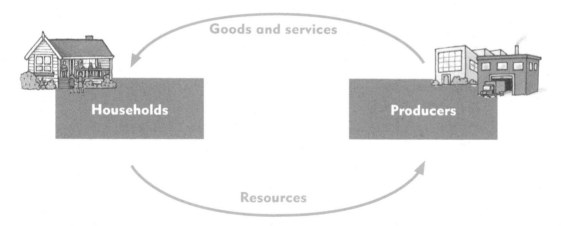

## Producer sector

It is easy to see that producers are reliant on households for their workers or labour. In Economics we assume that households own **all** resources, not just the labour. Households own all factors of production: land, labour, capital and entrepreneurship.

Consider the example of Richard Branson, an entrepreneur who owns several record companies and a chain of airlines. Branson is a householder and owns the whole company – planes, buildings, everything – but he does not own his workers. The workers have come from other households of consumers. All resources are ultimately owned by households.

ISBN: 9780170193955

**6**

Economics for NCEA Level One

ACTIVITY

1 Describe what is meant by each of these terms:
- labour
- land
- capital
- entrepreneurship

2 Copy and complete the table below to identify the main factor of production (resource) in each scenario. The first example has been done for you:

| | Scenario | Labour | Land | Capital | Entrepreneurship |
|---|---|---|---|---|---|
| | Tractors, fences and combine harvesters on a farm | | | ☒ | |
| 1 | Nurses, doctors and physiotherapists at a hospital | | | | |
| 2 | Orange roughy fish stocks | | | | |
| 3 | Graeme Hart, owner of *Reynolds Packaging Group* (RPG) | | | | |
| 4 | Vats, trucks and bottles at a winery | | | | |
| 5 | Carpenters, electricians and plumbers working on site | | | | |
| 6 | Sam Morgan, developer of *TradeMe* | | | | |

3 'Households own all resources'. Explain how this is true.

Households let firms use their resources, however, by doing this they expect to earn an income. There are specific terms we use in Economics for the income households earn from each resource.

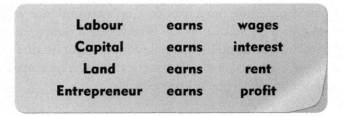

| | | |
|---|---|---|
| **Labour** | **earns** | **wages** |
| **Capital** | **earns** | **interest** |
| **Land** | **earns** | **rent** |
| **Entrepreneur** | **earns** | **profit** |

ISBN: 9780170193955

Although these terms are used by everyone in everyday speech, in this context they refer specifically to the 'return' earned by households for allowing firms to use their resources, a return that is paid as income. Households use this income to pay for the goods and services that they consume.

In turn, firms rely on households to provide the resources used in the production of goods and services and to purchase goods and services, which allows the producer to pay for the resources used in production. This interdependence can be shown on the circular flow model:

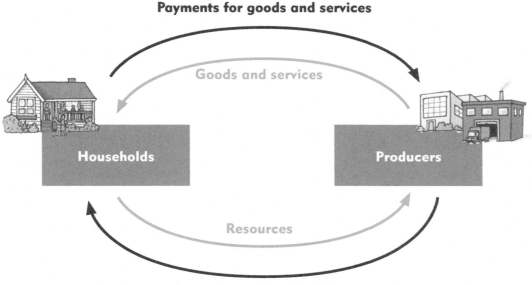

**Payments for goods and services**

Goods and services

Households

Producers

Resources

**Payment for resources**

The movement of goods and services and the resources (blue arrows) are actual flows. They are called **real flows**.

Household spending on goods and services and the payment for resources (brown arrows) are financial flows. They are called **money flows**.

The circular flow model is often drawn with only the money flows shown. The real flows can be inferred from the money flows.

**ACTIVITY**

1 Explain the difference between a real and a money flow.

2 Copy and complete the table below.

| Real flow | Money flow |
|---|---|
| goods and services | |
| resources | |

3 Draw a fully labelled two sector circular flow model showing both real and money flows.

ISBN: 9780170193955

Economics for NCEA Level One

ISBN: 9780170193955

**CASE STUDY**

# Unemployment

## 'The unemployment rate has surged to a nine-year high.'

A rise in unemployment means that fewer workers have jobs and so households have less income.

The money flow associated with workers wages is termed **payment for resources**. If fewer resources are employed then there is a smaller payment for resources.

This flow will impact on households first.

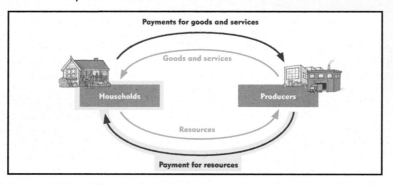

Household income is lower. Households respond to this by spending less on goods and services. This is the only flow out of households in the two sector model. Households spending less on goods and services affects the spending on goods and services flow.

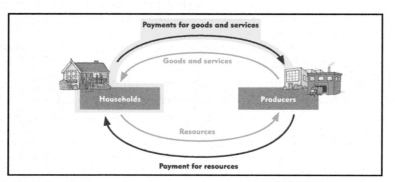

This will subsequently have an impact on firms. Households are spending less on goods and services, which reduces a firm's income. Firms may respond by spending less on resources. This is the only flow *out* of firms in the two sector model. This may mean firms reduce production, laying off workers or reducing work hours for workers.

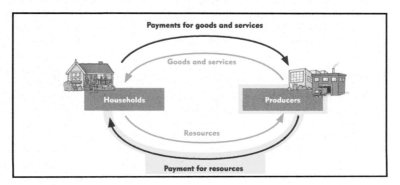

ACTIVITY

**1** Copy and complete the following table. All questions refer to a two sector circular flow model. The case study on page 170 has been rewritten in this format as the first example.

| Scenario | Directly affects ... (which flow) | Impacts on ... (which sector) | This sector responds by ... | This affects ... (which flow) | Which impacts on ... (which sector) | This sector responds by ... |
|---|---|---|---|---|---|---|
| Unemployment rises | Payments for resources | Households | Decreasing household spending on goods and services | Household spending on goods and services | Firms | Reducing spending on resources by: • Reducing production • Cutting workers hours • Laying off workers |
| 1 Signs NZ coming out of recession – households spending up at Christmas | | | | | | |
| 2 Job losses at the local mill | | | | | | |
| 3 Unemployment figures down for first time since global financial crisis | | | | | | |
| 4 Households tightening their belts as winter arrives | | | | | | |

Interdependence of sectors in the New Zealand economy

ISBN: 9780170193955

Economics for NCEA Level One

# 6

# 27 ▪ Three sector circular flow model

**By the end of this unit you will be able to:**

- Describe the financial sector service industry and explain its role in the economy.
- Define savings and investment.
- Draw the three-sector circular flow model using households, producers and the financial sector.
- Identify and explain injections and withdrawals on the circular flow model.
- Fully describe how an event can impact on the financial sector.
- Explain possible flow-on effects of such an event on at least two other sectors.

Households do not use all of their income to buy goods and services immediately. They can also save some of their income.

Savings is foregoing consumption now for consumption later. Instead of buying goods and services, funds are put aside to spend on goods and services later. Household generally save their income with a third party, usually banks.

Banks use the funds that households have saved and lend it to firms. Firms use the funds they have borrowed from the banks to increase their capital resources. Note that the language used here is very specialised. Remember the terms investment and capital have specific meanings when used in Economics.

Clearly this relationship needs to be shown in our circular flow model. We add another sector to produce a three sector model.

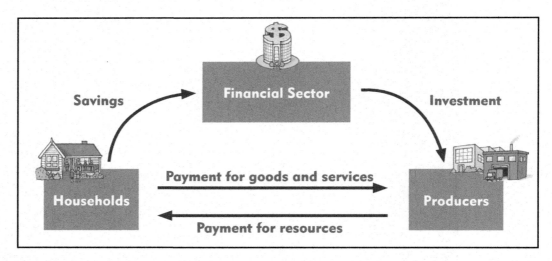

**Investment**
An increase in human-made resources.

**Capital**
Human-made resources.

The circular flow model only shows the money flows outlined above, and there are many other financial flows in real life. Households borrow from the banks and pay back these loans with interest. Firms sometimes borrow funds to do something other than increase capital, and must also repay loans with interest.

ISBN: 9780170193955

# Interest

Interest refers to return on capital, but it can also refer to the cost of borrowing funds. It is important to determine which context the word is being used in.

There are no real flows involving the financial sector. The financial sector is an intermediary between households and firms. They help households save surplus income and help firms borrow these funds.

From the model above you can see that savings takes money out of the circular flow. This is called a **withdrawal** from the circular flow. It means that instead of all household income being spent on goods and services, some is directed out of the circular flow and into the financial sector.

Investment is funds being put into the circular flow. This is an **injection** into the circular flow.

## Caught in the crunch

'Banks struggling to recover from multibillion-dollar losses on real estate are [stopping] loans to American businesses.'

Banks are decreasing lending to businesses following the credit crisis. The circular flow shows us that this will affect the flow of investment, which is decreasing. This flow will impact on firms first, the sector at the end of the flow.

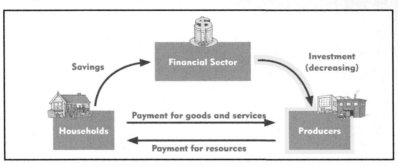

Producers have less investment funds. They will respond to this by spending less on resources. This is the only flow *out* of the producer sector in the three sector model. This could happen by reducing production, laying off workers or reducing working hours for workers. Firms' spending less on resources affects the **payment for resources** flow.

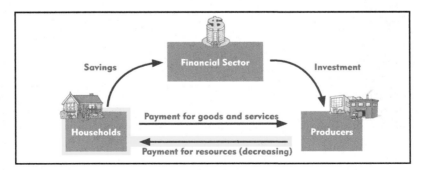

This will have an impact on households. Producers are spending less on resources, which reduces households' income. Households may respond by either spending less on goods and services, or reducing their savings. These are the only flows *out* of households in the three sector model.

ISBN: 9780170193955

**1** Copy and complete the following table. All questions refer to a three sector circular flow model. The case study on page 173 has been rewritten in this format as the first example.

| | Scenario | Directly affects ... (which flow) | Impacts on ... (which sector) | This sector responds by ... | This affects ... (which flow) | Which impacts on ... (which sector) | This sector responds by ... |
|---|---|---|---|---|---|---|---|
| | Banks curtail loans to business | Investment | Firms | Reducing spending on resources by: • Reducing production • Cutting workers hours • Laying off workers | Payment for resources | Households | Decreasing household spending on goods and services AND/OR decreasing savings |
| 1 | Households follow government advice and put money aside for retirement | | | | | | |
| 2 | Highest levels of unemployment yet recorded following global financial meltdown | | | | | | |
| 3 | Unemployment figures down for first time since global financial crisis | | | | | | |
| 4 | Banks announce increased interest rates on business lending | | | | | | |

ISBN: 9780170193955

Interdependence of sectors in the New Zealand economy

# 28 ▪ Four sector circular flow model

**By the end of this unit you will be able to:**

- Describe the government sector and explain its role in the economy.
- Describe transfer payments (social welfare spending and subsidies), taxes and government spending on goods and services.
- Include government injections and withdraws in the circular flow model.
- Fully describe the impact of an event on the government sector.
- Explain possible flow-on effects of such an event on at least two other sectors.

The government in New Zealand accounts for over 35% of all economic activity. It is a significant participant. The government collects taxes, for example PAYE, GST and company tax, as well as many other smaller taxes like excise taxes (a sales tax that is not placed on everything) for example, on cigarettes and alcohol.

From this revenue, the government makes several transfer payments:

- Subsidising certain goods and services, for example medicine or doctor's visits for under 6-year-olds
- Providing social welfare for New Zealand's most vulnerable citizens, for example the domestic purposes benefit, sickness benefit or superannuation scheme.
- Providing goods and services such as schools, hospitals and the police force.

The government also spends tax revenue on goods and services. This level of economic activity needs to be represented in our circular flow model, so we add another sector to show a four sector model.

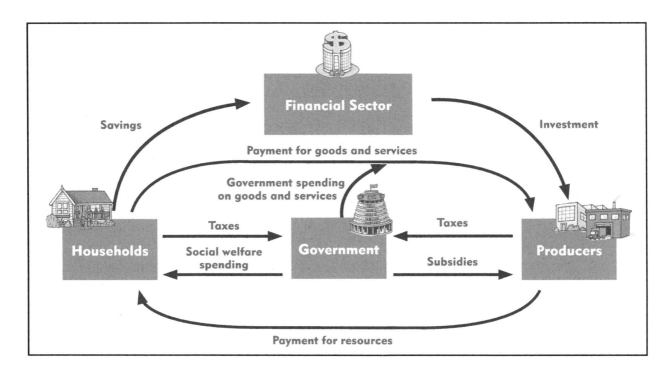

ISBN: 9780170193955

Economics for NCEA Level One

ISBN: 9780170193955

> **Transfer payment**
> A one-way payment of funds for which nothing is received in exchange.

In this four sector circular flow model, the transfer payments are social welfare spending on households and subsidies to firms. These transfer payments, together with the government spending on goods and services, are **injections** into the circular flow.

Taxes, on the other hand, are **withdrawals** from the circular flow. The tax from households to the government represents PAYE and the tax paid by firms to the government represents GST and company tax.

As our circular flow model has become more complicated, so too must our analysis of impacts and flow-on effects.

## ACTIVITY

Copy and fully label a four sector circular flow model.

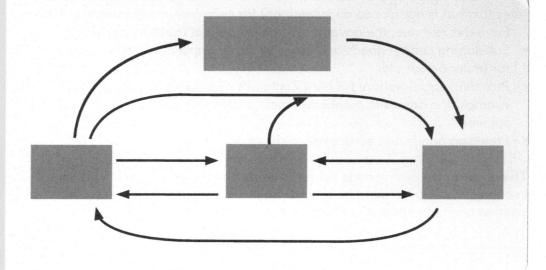

## CASE STUDY

### Interdependence and the circular flow model

This case study gives a sense of interrelationships and interdependence within the circular flow model. Each change causes another change and so on.

> **'... to drop the company tax rate to 30% is also a welcome step ...'**

The government has lowered company tax rates to 30%. The circular flow model tells us that this will affect the flow of taxes from firms to government: taxes are decreasing. This flow impacts both firms and the government.

# First line of reasoning: Firms

Firms have less tax to pay, which lowers costs and increases profitability. They will respond to this by spending more on resources. This is the only other flow *out* of firms in the four sector model. It could be achieved by increasing production, hiring more workers or paying overtime.

Firms' spending more on resources affects the payment for resources flow.

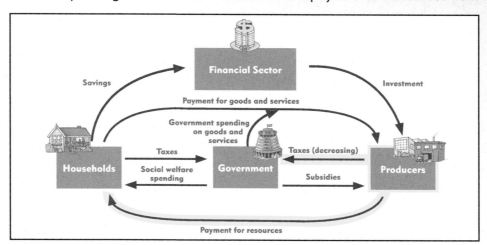

This will have an impact on households. Firms are spending more on resources, which increases households' income. Households may respond in many ways:

- Spending more on goods and services
- Increasing their savings
- Pay more taxes (PAYE increases because incomes have risen).

These are the only flows *out* of households in the four sector model.

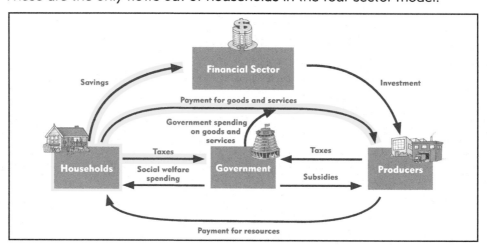

# Second line of reasoning: Government

The government is receiving less tax revenue from firms, and may respond to this by:

- Reducing government spending on goods and services
- Reducing transfer payments such as social welfare spending
- Removing subsidies
- Cutting benefits or reducing budgets for schools or hospitals.

ISBN: 9780170193955

These are the only flows *out* of government in the four sector model.

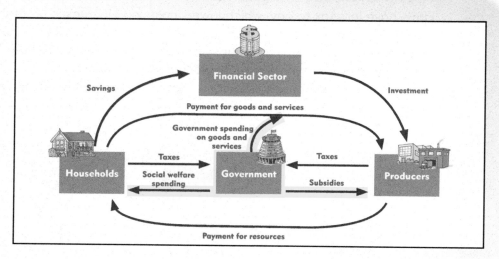

1 For each of the pairs of sectors below explain how they are interdependent. Include a specific example of this interdependence.
   a Households and producers.
   b Government and households.
   c Financial intermediaries and producers.

2 'Households decrease savings during economic downturn'.
   a Outline which flow this event affects initially.
   b Fully explain the impact that 'households using savings' has on the financial sector.
   c Fully explain the possible flow-on effect this has on firms.
   d Fully explain the possible flow-on effect this has on the government.

3 'The government increases spending on infrastructure to try to stimulate the economy'.
   a Outline which flow this event affects initially.
   b Fully explain the impact that 'government increases spending' has on households.
   c Fully explain the possible flow-on effect this has on the financial sector.
   d Fully explain the possible flow-on effect this has on the government.

ISBN: 9780170193955

# 29 ▪ Five sector circular flow model

Not all goods available in New Zealand are produced here. Some of these goods are made overseas and imported into the country. **Imports** are goods made overseas but sold in New Zealand.

Similarly, not all goods produced in New Zealand are sold here. Some goods are made here and exported overseas. **Exports** are goods made in New Zealand but sold overseas.

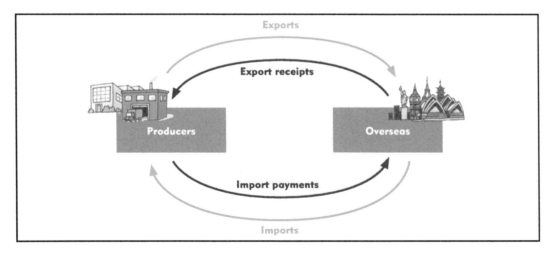

Exports and imports are **real flows**. They are the actual goods and services being traded internationally.

**Export receipts** are the payments from overseas firms to New Zealand firms for the goods and services exported overseas. They are a **money flow**.

**Import payments** are New Zealand producers' payments to overseas firms for the goods and services they have imported. They are also a **money flow**.

A circular flow model is most commonly shown with only money flows.

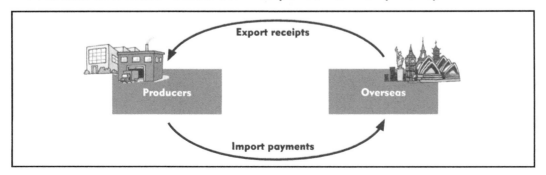

ISBN: 9780170193955

Economics for NCEA Level One

It is easy to become confused. Remember, export receipts are coming into New Zealand. (Exports, which are not shown, are leaving.)

Import payments are leaving New Zealand. (Imports, which are not shown, are entering the country.)

The income earned by selling New Zealand goods and services overseas is an **injection** into the circular flow.

The spending on goods and services from overseas is a **withdrawal** from the circular flow.

## ACTIVITY

**1** Copy and complete the following table, by ticking the correct column.

| | Scenario | Import Payments | | Export Receipts | |
|---|---|---|---|---|---|
| | | Increase | Decrease | Increase | Decrease |
| 1 | The Rugby World Cup (RWC) sees thousands of tourists coming to New Zealand | | | | |
| 2 | A fall in the number of Japanese car imports | | | | |
| 3 | An increase in New Zealand purchases of the latest computer product | | | | |
| 4 | Global crisis sees a fall in New Zealand logs being sent to Asia | | | | |
| 5 | New Zealanders going to Gallipoli to remember ANZAC Day reaches record numbers | | | | |
| 6 | Weta Digital is hired to create special effects on another US blockbuster | | | | |

These transactions can be incorporated into our circular flow model to give a better illustration of the New Zealand economy. We can use the model to help explain the flow-on effects of changes in one of the flows. Bear in mind that it shows only money flows.

ISBN: 9780170193955

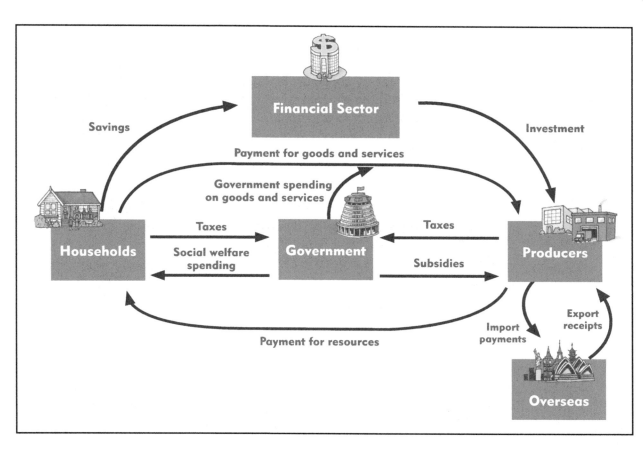

Unexpected events can also affect the import payments and export receipts flows.

CASE STUDY

## RWC draws more tourists

Imagine that these tourists are going to spend a lot of money in New Zealand. The firms sector is therefore receiving more and more income. This income for firms must flow *out*. Our model shows us there are three possible flows:

1 Increased income to **households**.
2 Increased tax to the **government** (from increased company tax).
3 Increased import payments paid to **overseas sector**.

Follow the flows to these sectors to see how they might respond to this change.

Since households have increased income, they could:

1 Increase spending on goods and services, which will affect firms.
2 Increase savings, which will affect the financial sector.
3 Increase taxes (PAYE from the increased income) and GST (from the increased spending), which will affect the government.

Since the government has increased tax income it could:

1 Increase government spending on goods and services. This could be mean increasing budgets for schools or hospitals.
2 Increase transfer payments, such as either social welfare spending (in dollar terms or the number who qualify) or subsidies (increasing the number of medicines that are subsidised).

ISBN: 9780170193955

ISBN: 9780170193955

# Eyjafjallajokull erupts!

The eruption under the Eyjafjallajokull glacier in 2010 threw large amounts of ash and smoke into the air. Flights across northern Europe were disrupted by volcanic ash drifting south and east from Iceland. Passengers heading to New Zealand were left stranded in London and around Europe, which meant less income earned in New Zealand from hosting these tourists.

> **'Air New Zealand says it lost about $2.5 million during the five days it was kept out of Europe due to an ash cloud from a volcano erupting in Iceland.'** (Source: www. reuters.com)

> **'The money was spent bussing stranded passengers in some cases and accommodating them in others.'** (Source: www.radionz.co.nz)

Export receipts decreased. There was a smaller injection into the economy.

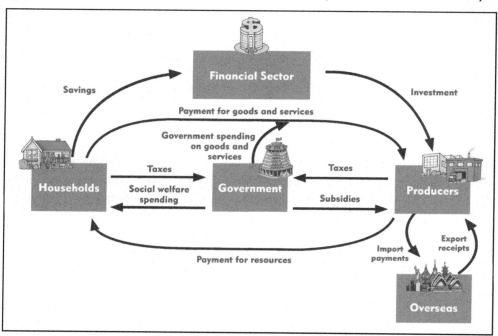

Looking at our circular flow model we can see that if firms are earning fewer export receipts they are going to have lower payments to households. There might be less work available for tourist operators, hotel employees and local restaurants, for example.

As their income falls this could in turn decrease the level of savings householders are able to make, or lower the level of household spending on goods and services.

As a result of this, the tax revenue earned by the government from GST and PAYE would also decrease.

Interdependence of sectors in the New Zealand economy

1 For each of the scenarios listed below, outline one impact on the sector identified in brackets.
   a Tourist dissatisfaction with Europe's high price sees increased numbers of travellers to New Zealand (Producers).
   b The US relaxes tariffs on New Zealand steel (Producers).
   c OCR (interest rates) rise (Households).
   d New employment legislation sees workers incomes fall (Households).
   e A loosening of the government purse strings sees social welfare spending increase (Households).

2 For each scenario above outline the flow-on effects for two other sectors.

3 Copy and complete the five sector circular flow model (ensure your arrows are pointing the right way).

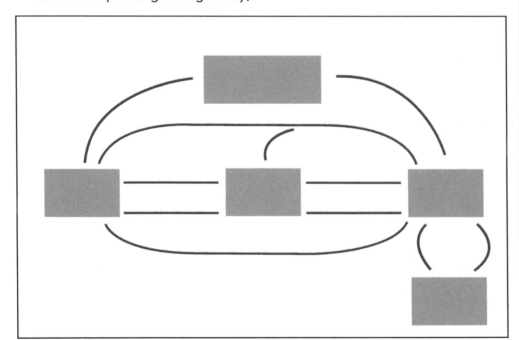

ISBN: 9780170193955

# Glossary

**backward vertical integration:** merging with or taking over a business at an earlier stage of the production process

**business expansion:** when businesses increase their scale of operations by starting up, merging with, or taking over other businesses

**capital good:** human-made goods that are used in the production of other goods and services, for example bulldozers, computers

**capital intensive production:** a method of production where relatively more capital resources than labour are used in the production process

**central government:** group of politically elected representatives that govern a nation

*ceteris paribus:* all other things remaining the same

**change in supply:** a change in the amount of a good or service that a firm is willing and able to produce, at every price level. Results from a change in non-price factors.

**choice:** a decision made from a selection of options

**circular flow model:** a representation of the interdependent relationships in an economy

**collective good:** a good that is provided out of taxation

**commercial goals:** a financial reason for being in business, for example, to maximise profits or to increase market share of the business

**complementary goods:** goods that are traditionally used together, for example a digital camera and a memory card

**consumer:** anyone who uses goods or services

ISBN: 9780170193955

**consumer good:** physical items that are used by individuals or groups in the household sector, for example, a cellphone

**cost of production:** amount paid for inputs in the production process

**demand:** the quantity of a good or service a consumer is willing and able to buy at a range of prices at a certain time

**demand curve:** a graph showing information about a consumers demand for a particular good or service over a range of prices

**demand schedule:** a table showing information about a consumer's demand for a particular good or service over a range of prices at a certain time

**demerit goods:** goods and services that the government believes are bad for you, for example cigarettes

**depreciation:** when capital resources become worn out and begin to lose value and productivity

**diseconomies of scale:** as the size of operations rises, average costs rise

**disposable income:** the funds remaining after taxes are paid

**diversification:** increasing the range of goods and services that a business produces; expanding a business into something different

**division of labour:** separating a production process into specific parts

**economies of scale:** as the size of operations rises, average costs fall

**entrepreneur:** the decision maker and risk taker

**equilibrium point:** the stable point in a market where quantity demanded and which quantity supplied are equal

**external non-price factors:** factors outside of the firm which affects supply and the firm may have little or no control over, for example, environmental issues, legal requirements, cultural obligations

**exchange rate:** the value of one currency in relation to the currency of another country

**excise tax:** an additional tax that may be added to the price of a good or service, particularly those the government considers are bad for consumers, for example cigarettes

**firm:** a single business or producer

**flow-on effects:** implications for other people resulting from decisions that others make

**forward vertical integration:** merging with or taking over a business at a later stage of the production process

ISBN: 9780170193955

ISBN: 9780170193955

**goods:** physical objects
**GST:** Goods and Services Tax, an example of an indirect or sales tax

**horizontal integration:** merging with or taking over another business at the same stage in the production process
**household:** a group of consumers who live under one roof
**households:** all consumers in an economy (see **circular flow**)

**income:** funds either earned or unearned that are received by a person or household
**industry:** a group of firms in the same line of business
**inferior goods:** goods that are considered of a lower quality or that are used by those on lower incomes. When income increases, demand for inferior goods falls
**integrate:** joining businesses together
**interdependence:** relying on each other
**interest:** the return for capital
**interest rates:** the cost to the producer of borrowing funds
**intermediate good:** a finished good that is only useful when it is used in the production process of another good
**investment:** increase in capital resources

**labour:** human work or effort (excluding the risk taker)
**labour intensive production:** a method of production where relatively more labour than machinery is used in the production process
**law of demand:** 'as the price falls, the quantity demanded increases, *ceteris paribus*, vice versa'
**law of supply:** 'as the price rises, the quantity supplied increases, *ceteris paribus*, vice-versa'
**local government:** regional authorities, for example, city councils

**market:** any place or situation where buyers and sellers interact to exchange goods and services
**market forces:** pressure on price and quantity in the market, which comes from the combination of consumer need for goods and services and the need of

producers to sell their goods and services, otherwise known as the invisible hand

**market share:** the proportion of total sales of the good or service that is made by a particular producer

**means:** personal resources we can use to satisfy our needs and wants, for example our time, skills, money, family or whanau, iwi or hapu

**merge:** when two (or more) businesses decide to join together for their mutual benefit

**merit good:** goods and services that the government considers good for consumers

**natural resources:** anything that occurs naturally on land, in the sea, in the air. For example, renewable (eg. sunlight) and non-renewable (eg. fossil fuels)

**need:** what we must have in order to survive, also known as necessities, for example food, clothing, shelter

**non-commercial goals:** being in business for reasons other than financial reasons, for example, personal reasons

**non-price competition:** using any other method other than price to attract customers

**opportunity cost:** the next best choice that is foregone when a decision is made

**PAYE:** Pay As You Earn, the New Zealand government tax on workers income

**price competition:** being the lowest priced supplier

**price maximum:** the highest price that a good or service may be sold for, also called a price ceiling

**price minimum:** the lowest price a good or service may be sold for, also called price floor

**price war:** when firms lower prices below cost in an effort to drive competition out of the market

**private sector producer:** a business owned by an individual or group from the household sector

**producer:** an individual or firm that supplies a good or a service

**product differentiation:** when a good or service is made to appear different from similar products on the market while making no actual changes to it

**product variation:** making actual or real changes to a good or service

**production:** the process of transforming inputs into goods or services

**production costs:** the cost of inputs into the production process, for example wages, raw materials

**productivity:** output per unit of input

ISBN: 9780170193955

**profit:** the difference between the income earned by a firm and the expenses incurred

**protectionism:** when governments protect local producers from competition by overseas producers

**public sector producer:** a producer owned by the government

**quota:** a limit on the quantity of a good that can be imported

**rates:** payment by property owners to their local government in exchange for services, for example, rubbish collection

**recycle:** to use resources in other production processes

**RMA:** The Resource Management Act is a New Zealand law put in place to manage the use of natural and physical resources including land, air and water

**resources:** human, capital or natural inputs into the production process

**sales tax:** an indirect tax or tax on consumption

**savings:** the proportion of income not spent

**scarcity:** when needs and wants are greater than the ability to satisfy those needs and wants

**service:** something that is done for you, for example a hair cut

**shortage:** when quantity demanded is higher than the quantity supplied, also called excess demand

**specialisation:** to focus on a particular area of production

**State Owned Enterprise:** firms owned by central government that are run like private sector businesses, with a view to making a profit

**subsidy:** a transfer payment from the government to producers that has the effect of lowering their costs of production

**substitute goods:** goods that can traditionally be used in place of each other, for example butter and margarine

**supply:** the quantity of a good or service that a producer is willing and able to produce at a range of prices at a certain time

**supply curve:** a graph showing a firms ability to supply a good or service over a range of prices

**supply schedule:** a table showing a firm's ability to supply a particular good or service over a range of prices at a certain time

**surplus:** unsold goods and services, when the quantity supplied is higher than the quantity demanded, also called excess supply

ISBN: 9780170193955

**takeover:** when a dominant firm buys a controlling share in another firm

**tariff:** a tax that governments may place on imported goods

**tastes:** when goods become more fashionable, or our preferences move towards them, the demand for them increases, and vice-versa

**technology:** capital goods, processes and various methods of production that a firm uses

**values:** principles and beliefs that we consider to be important

**vertical integration:** merging with or taking over a business at a different stage of the production process

**voluntary organisations:** usually a non-profit organisation that aims to satisfy a social need, for example World Vision

ISBN: 9780170193955

# Index

ISBN: 9780170193955